WRITER'S UTOPIA FORMULA REPORT

by
JERRY BUCHANAN

WRITER'S UTOPIA
FORMULA REPORT

COPYRIGHT © 1973, 1975, 1977

By Jerry M. Buchanan

Sixth printing .... April, 1977

All rights reserved internationally. No part of this publication may be reproduced, stored in a retrieval system, or transmitted, in any form or by any means, electronic, mechanical, photo-copying, recording, or otherwise, without the prior written permission of the author/publisher.

Printed at:
Graphics Arts Center
2000 N. W. Wilson,
Portland, Oregon 97209
United States of America

Press On

Nothing in the world can take the place of persistence. Talent will not; nothing is more common than unsuccessful men with talent. Genius will not; unrewarded genius is almost a proverb. Education will not; the world is full of educated derelicts. Persistence and determination alone are omnipotent.

The Golden Rule

Confucianism

    What you don't want done to yourself, don't do to others. —Sixth Century b.c.

Buddhism

    Hurt not others with that which pains thyself. —Fifth Century b.c.

Jainism

    In happiness and suffering, in joy and grief, we should regard all creatures as we regard our own self, and should therefore refrain from inflicting upon others such injury as would appear undesirable to us if inflicted upon ourselves. —Fifth Century b.c.

Zoroastrianism

    Do not do unto others all that which is not well for oneself. —Fifth Century b.c.

Classical Paganism

    May I do to others as I would that they should do unto me. *Plato*—Fourth Century b.c.

Hinduism

    Do naught to others which if done to thee would cause thee pain. *Mahabharata*—Third Century b.c.

Judaism

    What is hateful to yourself, don't do to your fellow man. *Rabbi Hillel*—First Century b.c.

Christianity

    Whatsoever ye would that men should do to you, do ye even so to them. *Jesus of Nazareth*—First Century a.d.

Sikhism

    Treat others as thou wouldst be treated thyself. —Sixteenth Century a.d.

Perhaps the oldest ethical proposition of distinctly universal character

Let's Get Acquainted!

Hello, I'm Jerry Buchanan, author/publisher/salesman/entrepreneur. There have been a few dozen other occupations in between 17 and 50, but those will do for now. I thought you might like to get to know me before you plunge into my book.

Well, for you astrology buffs, I'm a double Sagittarius with Pisces rising and moon, Mercury and Venus in Capricorn.

For those who judge a man by his religion... I'm a student of all religions and still seriously searching for Truth in its purest essence. Meanwhile I try to let the Golden Rule guide me in all affairs. I am tolerant of the belief of others but I resent it when you come to me with what you believe to be the simple answer.

But all this is beside the point. You are probably much more interested in finances, right? O.K., I have been as broke as the next guy, more often than the next guy. I know what it is to be stuck in Miami, Florida without a dime, at 40, and have to take a job delivering the Miami Morning Herald to survive and save for a bus ticket back home. I know what it is to go on state unemployment compensation, yes and even stand in line for food stamps.

I also know what it is to own my own yacht, country estate and acreage; Lincoln Continentals, real estate holdings, investments, a loving, young and beautiful wife and all the creature comforts. I know the wonderful feeling of complete financial security, even in hard times. Best of all, I know the exhilarating feeling of being my own boss; working out of my own home at a business I own and control completely. A business that is the result of many years of "trial & error" testing and re-testing. Where did I get the money to begin? I stole it. Yes, I stole it from my own salary. Instead of buying life and auto insurance, as any ordinary man would, I gambled the money away on my own ideas. I stole it from my "new car" savings, and drove the old buggy longer. I did without booze, movies, night clubs, restaurants, cigarettes!! This book will save you from many costly errors along the way, but you'll still need to make sacrifices if you need start-up capital.

I must caution you, if you are one who pre-judges a book by its cover, or its size . . . don't judge this one that way! I have purposely kept it thin. Your time is worth money. I considered that. So, I took Ernest Hemmingway's advice. He said: *"The first and most important thing of all, at least for writers today, is to strip language clean, to lay it bare down to the bone."*

If you are wise enough to appreciate that, then you may go far with the foundation I have outlined for you here. Consider this book worthy of a place of highest honors on your book shelf. It could, in time, come to be regarded as the cornerstone upon which you built your whole retirement fortune!

JERRY BUCHANAN
VANCOUVER, WASHINGTON

The drawing on facing page shows some of my favorite books. Someone once said: *"Let me spend 15 minutes browsing through a man's personal library and I'll tell you all about that man."*

My home library is much too vast to have been included in its entirety in that small caricature, but since I'm a collector of famous quotations, maxims, proverbs, sayings and aphorisms, perhaps the following favorites will help you to know me better.

"Every book salesman is an advance agent for culture and for better citizenship; for education and for the spread of intelligence."
- - Dr. Frank Crane

"The writer does the most who gives his reader the most knowledge and takes from him the least time."
- - Sydney Smith

"It is indisputably evident that a great part of every man's life must be employed in collecting materials for the exercise of genius. Invention, strictly speaking, is little more than a new combination of those images which have been previously gathered and deposited in the memory; nothing can come of nothing: he who has laid up no materials can produce no combinations. The more extensive, therefore, your acquaintance is with the works of those who have excelled, the more extensive will be your powers of invention, and, what may appear still more like a paradox, the more original will be your conceptions.
- - Sir Joshua Reynolds

"Tell your story as succinctly as you can, then cut it by a third, at least. If you think it cannot be done, take a novel you enjoyed and compare it, page by page with the 'Reader's Digest Condensed Books' version. That will show you it can be done, and often to the best advantage."
- - Frederick Forsyth, author of
Day Of The Jackal

We have tried our best to incorporate all these philosophies into the writing and publishing of this book. It is our hope that the concepts we have presented will lend a fresh surge of enthusiasm to your own writing aspirations.

Jerry Buchanan

Vancouver, Washington

THE FIRST SECRET OF SUCCESS IS IN CHOOSING A FIELD THAT WILL HOLD YOUR INTEREST AND ENTHUSIASM

The person who has found a way to earn a living doing that which he would do anyway, provided he did not *have* to work for a living, is quite possibly the luckiest person in the world! Many of my buyers are up in years and past the age where they are likely to begin a new career **if it requires long hours of school to learn how to do it.** These people have a lifetime of valuable experience and knowledge they would like to be able to pass on to others before they pass on to their reward. If they can make a comfortable income in the process, why all the better! Many of them have dabbled in the writing trade for years but few have credits for their work. Perhaps a few articles have been published in their local paper or in a trade journal but the pay, if any, was small and soon spent and forgotten. Here is a way for them to write on a hundred different subjects and sell every single article they can produce while helping their fellow man through the dissemination of valuable "How-To" information. Most important, the renewed interest in life and the feeling of being needed will add many years to their lifespan. Happy, productive, useful years.

When this book was still in typed manuscript form, a lady in La Grange, Illinois wrote the following: *"Dear Jerry, I have been bubbling over with happiness since I received your Writer's Utopia Formula and more so since joining TOWERS CLUB, USA! You do inspire me so! Never again will I be bored or lonely. Just think - - at last, I'll have enough interests to last for the remainder of my life!"*

Letters such as that one (and my files are overflowing with them) make me feel very humble and yet extremely proud that I have, at last, found something to sell that I don't need to feel ashamed of. If you've been a commissioned salesman for very long, you know what I'm talking about.

TABLE OF CONTENTS

PRESS ON	i
THE GOLDEN RULE	ii
LET'S GET ACQUAINTED	iii
THE FIRST SECRET OF SUCCESS	vi
THIS IS THE FORMULA	1
CATEGORIES	3
SUBJECTS	4, 5, & 6
UNIVERSAL INTEREST	6
IMPORTANT!!!	10
RESEARCHING YOUR SUBJECTS	10
HOW TO BECOME A RESEARCH EXPERT	11
SOME VERY IMPORTANT ADDRESSES	13
HOW TOWERS CLUB, U.S.A. WAS BORN	15
THE MOLES & GOPHERS STORY	16
STOP AND DECIDE. STOP OR GO ON.	18
I BARGAINED WITH LIFE FOR A PENNY (Poem)	19
BEGIN: PART TWO	20
TO WHOM DO WE SELL WHAT WE'VE WRITTEN?	21
HERE'S WHAT YOU DO	22
DIRECT RESPONSE SELLING	23
TESTING YOUR ADS	25
PSYCHOLOGY OF SELLING BY MAIL	26
TWO METHODS OF M. O. ADVERTISING	28
JOE AND BETTY KARBO	29
THE MILLIONAIRES WHO'VE MADE IT THIS WAY 28 --- 32
WHO'S MAKING THE MOST MONEY (Religion)	33
FIRST AMENDMENT AND KIRBY HENSLEY	34
JUDGE BATTEN'S LANDMARK DECISION	35
A BAG OF TOOLS	36
YOUR OWN BEST WRITING STYLE (R.D. reprint)	37
"I CAN'T SPEL VARY GUD"	41
FINDING THE TIME TO WRITE	41
THE ART OF USING EMOTIONAL APPEAL	44
WRITING AND PLACING CLASSIFIED ADS	45
CHOOSING A GOOD TITLE	46
THE CARLA EMERY SUCCESS STORY	47
WHERE DO YOU PLACE THOSE ADS?	47

TABLE OF CONTENTS

THREE GOOD ADVERTISING AGENCIES	48
MORE ON COMPOSING A GOOD CLASSIFIED AD	49
START YOUR OWN ADVERTISING AGENCY	51
"ONE PICTURE IS WORTH ---" ILLUSTRATE IT !	52
HARRY VOLK ART STUDIO	53
PREPARING "CAMERA - READY COPY"	54
YOUR OFFER AND YOUR PRICE -- ALL IMPORTANT	55
MONEY - BACK GUARANTEES & PRICING	56
BUSINESS LICENSES & TAXES	59
COPYRIGHT PROCEDURE	59
IMPORTANCE OF LETTERHEAD STATIONERY	60
IF YOU DON'T KNOW HOW TO TYPE	60
BIG MONEY IN PUBLISHING NEWSLETTERS !	61
KEEP THOSE RECORDS !	63
WHEN ORDERING THOSE MAGAZINE ADS	64
SAMPLE INSERTION - ORDER FORM	65
"OPPORTUNITY" TYPE MAGAZINES	66
STANDARD RATE & DATA ADDRESS ! ! !	66
THE MASTER SALESMAN	67
OPPORTUNITIES . . . THE RIVER OF LIFE	69
WORKING WITH WORDS -- SALESMAN'S STOCK IN TRADE	70
GETTING STARTED	72
CART BEFORE THE HORSE METHODOLOGY	72
MINI-COURSE IN MAIL ORDER PROCEDURES	73
TOWERS CLUB, U.S.A.	77
ASSOCIATE RESEARCH EXCHANGE PROGRAM	79
WHEN WE BUY A BOOK	81
THE EXTRA NEEDED INGREDIENT (Salesmanship)	82
TOWERS BOOK SALES DIVISION	83
COPYWRITER'S CREED & OUR INNER CIRCLE	84
HOW TO ORDER FROM US	85

You purchased this book to learn how I make a good living writing and selling words, even though I have never had a single day's formal training in the art of writing for pay. I did finish high school; I did have two old maid teachers take a liking to me. One taught English Literature and the other taught Typing. That was the total extent of my formal training and I didn't attempt any commercial writing until many, many years after high school. In fact I was in my early forties.

You purchased this book because I told you "anyone with a modicum of wits could do equally as well as I have, using my formula. I repeat now, it isn't your writing skill that makes this work . . . it's your knowledge of the subject, and if you don't even have that, I'll teach you where to look to get it! The world is full of expert typists who will put your words into saleable form, once you have created them, at very little cost to you. I'll tell you how to find and hire them to do your tedious work.

PART ONE
This is the Formula...

I choose the subject of every report I write according to the following specifications. Each must:

(a) be a "How-To-Do-It" article,

(b) have a reasonably broad popular appeal, at least to a certain segment of the population. For instance, farmers, teen-agers, gardeners, camera enthusiasts, retirees, home-makers opportunity seekers, yachtsmen, salesmen, etc. Any group large enough that some magazine publisher has seen fit to publish a magazine about them or for them. If my subject turns out to be one that appeals to virtually everybody, then I have hit on a "gem of rare value."

(c) be about something that isn't taught in most established institutions of higher learning (There can be exceptions here).

(d) contain common problems, the solution to which will either save the reader time or money; teach him how to make **more money** or **easier money**; help him achieve some emotionally oriented goal he craves desperately **or** help him avoid an experience he fears to a great degree, (fire, robbery, rejection, business failure, divorce, illness, death, etc).

1

If these specifications seem unduly restrictive to you, at first, put your mind at ease! There is virtually **no limit** to the subjects you could think of. I'm certain that in the short space of one hour, I could fill a typewritten page with suitable categories **and so could *you!*** When we had finished, I doubt if there would be more than one or two duplications between your list and mine unless our mutual ESP rapport happened to be extremely strong.

CHOOSING THE PROPER SUBJECT

Begin making a list of suitable subjects as soon as possible. Carry a scratch tablet with you wherever you go. Keep it handy, especially when you are reading the paper or a magazine. Always keep it beside you in the car since most of us get many good ideas while driving, for some strange reason. Keep that pad by your bed. Ideas will come when you are relaxed and not thinking about anything in particular. In this enlightened age, many of us have already learned how to tap the sub-conscious mind for original ideas, but for those of you who haven't, it is really quite simple. Just before you drop off to sleep each night, visualize, as vividly as you are able, the problem you want solved. Go over every detail in your mind. Make notes on that bedside pad, if it helps. Let yourself drift off to sleep while trying to solve the problem. Next morning, the second you awaken, grab for that pad again and write down the first thing that pops into your mind, no matter how silly or extreme it may seem at the moment. It will be your creative sub-conscious mind, trying to tell you something. Later in the day, after coffee (or whatever) go back and read again what you have written. A good idea is sure to come out of it. **ACT ON IT!**

No problem ever comes to you for which the answer is not already within you.

Here's a good way to condition your mind before starting to compile your list of possible subjects to write about. Ask yourself what subjects **everybody in the world** has in common. You'll come up with a few. There's childhood, a body (and all its component parts), and there's death. Everyone has a body, a childhood and, eventually, everyone experiences death. Everyone is born, lives a while and then dies. What else can you think of that is common to **everyone?**

Next, make a list which includes almost everyone. What subjects are of interest to almost everyone? Well, let's see. There's **money**! That is probably one of the most universally interesting subjects. There's **good health** which is probably next in line. There's **romance, human acceptance, pride, occupation, religion, music, pleasures of the five senses, hobbies**; how many more can you think of? Make your own list and surprise yourself at how long this list can grow. What you are doing here is building *categories*. Under each *category* are many *subjects* for you to research.

Use the next page.
List your favorite categories & subjects.

CATEGORIES

_____
_____
_____
_____
_____
_____

SUBJECTS

Now that you have listed several general categories and several general subjects under each category you should begin to see how easy it is going to be. *Note:* it makes absolutely no difference how many times before somebody has written a book on the subject **you** finally choose to write about.

Information (book) buyers are a little like squirrels. Once they have realized their instinct for gathering nuts (bits of information on a particular subject) they continue to collect everything that even **looks** like a nut. I once dug up a ground squirrel's nest on our property by accident. Among the store of nuts were 13 glass marbles the children had lost and even one **steel ball bearing!**

Who listens once listens twice.

Look in your own home library. Aren't there several books on one particular subject? Of course there are. My own library is no different. Readers are the same the world over in this respect.

Now that you have made your initial lists, let's take a look at what a few others, who are already marketing their writings my way, have written and sold.

make Money FORTUNE
MAKE MONEY FROM A SMALL GARDEN
HOW TO APPEAR IN T.V. COMMERCIALS
SEWING FOR PROFIT BY MAIL
BUYING AND SELLING STAMPS AND COINS
MAKE A FORTUNE COLLECTING JUNK
HOW TO SELL NEWSPAPER CLIPPINGS
HOW TO START A GREETING CARD COMPANY
LOSE WEIGHT WITHOUT DIETING
RAISING RABBITS FOR BIG MONEY
HOW TO PUBLISH & SELL YOUR SONGS
MY PATENTED RECIPE FOR - - -

1,000 WAYS TO SELL YOUR PHOTOGRAPHS
HOW TO WIN NATIONAL CONTESTS
HOW TO BECOME AN ANIMAL TRAINER
HOW TO BECOME A GHOST WRITER
HOW TO CREATE AND SELL HUMOR
MAKE BIG MONEY RAISING HERBS AT HOME
GROW BONZAI TREES FOR FUN & PROFIT
MAKE MONEY WITH YOUR TAPE RECORDER
MAKE MONEY RAISING EARTH WORMS
FOREIGN JOB OPPORTUNITES (current)
TEST YOUR OWN I. Q. AT HOME
HOW TO PREPARE YOUR WILL
SAVE THOUSANDS BUYING A HOME
HOW TO QUIT SMOKING EASILY

This list does not even begin to scratch the surface of subjects people will pay money to find out about. I listed them only to prime your mental pump for more ideas to come. Spend an hour at your favorite magazine stand. Read only the titles of articles printed on the covers of almost every magazine. Notice that you will almost never read a cover without a "How–To" title printed there to stimulate sales. That's your first clue that I am giving you valuable information here. All those publishers can't be wrong! But let this next sentence sink in! **You will sell your articles for dollars per word instead of pennies. That's right!** Why? Because you are not going to write the **shallow** articles those publishers buy and you are not going to sell the **in-depth** articles you *do* write to those publishers. You are, instead, going to copyright your own material and sell it **over and over again at full retail prices directly to the consumer!** More about that later.

CHOOSE A SUBJECT WITH UNIVERSAL INTEREST

Have you any idea what was the commercially best selling nonfiction book ever written? I'll tell you. It was *"The Common Sense Book of Baby and Child Care"* by **Dr. Benjamin Spock.** First published in New York in May, 1946, it had sold **23 million copies** by January 1972. Dr. Spock's book was written with a ball point pen and typed by his wife (a silk heiress).

Why do you suppose this book holds such a record? Remember on pages 2 and 3 we were discussing and listing what subjects all men had in common? We agreed that every person has

The Complete Book Of Pregnancy, Baby and Child Care

a childhood, a body and, eventually a death. For every child born, there is at least one parent and most often two. Children, then, are one of the most common subjects a writer could choose to write about. Death could be another, but it is not nearly as popular a subject as little babies. For every baby born there is a mother who dotes on its every gurgle and smile. What a ready made, universal topic to choose to write about!

Remember the business minded novelist who wanted to know what subjects sold best in fiction? Through some diligent research he learned they were, in order: **Abraham Lincoln, dogs and doctors.** Armed with this knowledge he sat down and wrote a novel and called it *"Abraham Lincoln's Doctor's Dog."* True story or not, this enterprising author had the right idea!

The human body offers an abundance of subjects to write about. It's a subject that is universally interesting. Everybody has a body and every body needs a lot of care and attention. The older we grow, the more attention it demands, in fact. Now, of course, our dear American Medical Association will jump on you if you start dispensing medical advice that could injure or maim your reader in any way. The way to get around that, if you intend to sell your grandmother's favorite remedy for t' is to print in large, bold letters, at the beginning, t a doctor and that the reader should first consul they have what you are going to suggest they cur grandmother's remedy. That's called *"playing* **Game."**

I can tell you that the subject of **"How to make lots of money"** is first in line of importance in the universality scale. Everyone would like to know more about making or saving money. Write a good report on this subject and **I guarantee you will soon be rich!** Religion can be a very appealing topic but it must be handled very cleverly and adroitly in order for it to prove a profitable subject. Although I have deep religious convictions, I wouldn't touch it with the proverbial "ten foot pole." On the other hand, I might plunge right in there with the loosely related subject of the **occult** because that is one of the most popular subjects afield today! Look at the **Rosicrucians**. They must be clearing a fortune to continue to run full back cover ads in almost every known magazine published! I visited their grounds in San Jose, California in 1959 and could not see where all that money had been spent on fancy trappings, although the real estate itself must be worth millions. Someone will no doubt write in and bring me up to date on this.

I can remember when **ASTARA** first began. I received literature from them in the beginning, many years ago. It was no more professionally done than my first W.U. Report. As I remember, it was mimeographed, in fact. "Here", I thought, "is another pair of typical California 'Occult Nuts' trying to do a poor imitation of the Rosicrucians. I wish them luck." Today I'm willing to bet the couple who started it are more than wealthy. They're making a fortune selling valuable information by mail!

It seems most beginners with Writer's Utopia Formula are fired with the enthusiasm to write their first report but immediately become bogged down when actually settling on the first subject. They starve-out for lack of an original idea. This really amazes me because I get them daily, out of thin air. More than I could ever hope to write up. Here are just a few that occur to me as I sit, typing this rough draft:

1. Which states permit acupuncture legally? List of clinics in those states with names and addresses.

2. DMSO, the miracle drug the FDA won't release. Cures arthritis, lumbago and even mental retardation. Write complete story plus where it is available. (Either Mexico or from your local veterinarian if you tell him it's for your animal).

Sell a collection of legal forms that fit one business. For instance, an advertising agency; a rental property owner; a job placement bureau; a resume writing service; a freelance photographer's forms for models, etc.

4. How to train your mind to be clairvoyant. How to be precognicient (see into the future). How to experiment with psychokinesis, (the power of mind over matter). How to tap the treasure of your own subconscious mind, etc.

5. All about self-divorce, self made wills, self incorporating, self-bankruptcy, etc., all without attorney's fees.

6. How to start a "friendship-by-mail" correspondence club.

7. How to start and operate an animal obedience school.

8. All about high funeral costs and how to avoid them.

9. The inside story of cancer cures the A.M.A. won't tell us about.

10. Vitamins, minerals and salts. Which ones are said to cure which ailments. A compendium for quick reference.

11. How to buy vitamin pills and capsules wholesale and sell them retail for unbelievably large mark-up profits!

12. How to raise your child to become a genius without robbing him/her of a normal, happy childhood.

13. How to turn your photography hobby into a paying proposition. 1,000 markets that will buy your best photos.

14. How to meet the proper life-mate without frequenting drinking establishments. The fifty most likely places and situations.

15. Sure-fire betting formulas for Las Vegas or the race track.

I admit, one or two of these are already being done, but don't let that scare you out if you have a plan or remedy. Who buys once will buy again and again! And most of these are subjects even I would pay money to know about (although I already know a little about each one).

So . . . now I have given you another 15 good idea starters. Don't let me hear from you that you just can't seem to think of a good subject on which to begin. The **ether** is **full** of ideas, just waiting for someone like you to grab up and run with. Pick just one, **put on your blinders and go to it!** That's all there is to it.

IMPORTANT!

Within your mind and memory is stored an astounding abundance of useful information you have gathered over a lifetime! It's already there! You've used it many times in the course of your own life. THINK ABOUT IT! We humans have a tendency to crave useful knowledge, and yet, after we have gained it, we tend to write it off as "not too valuable" because we tend to believe that almost everybody else must know it also and we were just late learning about it. THIS IS A FALSE PREMISE! When you change your thinking on this one vital point you are already halfway to the gold!

RESEARCHING YOUR SUBJECT

Once I have chosen an appropriate subject, I do not rely on my own knowledge, alone, to fill the report. I take what I already know, verify it, and then add everything else that others have learned about it as well. This requires some research . . . some hours spent at the library, and though this can be considered hard work to some, I guarantee that the hours thus spent will pay you **far more than any hourly wage job you ever held in your life.**

Someone once said, and wisely, that if you wish to become a rich person, find a need and fill it! In this case, the need is specific "How-To-Do-It" information, coupled with the fact that most people are either too busy or too lazy to do their own research. They are happy to have you do it for them and will pay heavy money for the task!

Now you shouldn't let the word "**research**" scare you ply another word for "reading", making notes and the. ing the gathered material in proper sequence. If you don make notes, take a pocket full of dimes to the library and photocopy machine. That's what I do.

Do your research thoroughly enough and the final written report will almost write itself! Of course, you cannot copy word for word from someone else's material. That is called plagiarism. But ideas cannot be copyrighted . . . only patented . . . and then, only if they are unique. There's an old saw that goes: "Copy the words of one man and you are a plagiarist - - copy the ideas of many and it is called research."

I can't stress strongly enough, the importance of doing a complete and thorough job of research on each project. Cover every facet of your subject. Search every nook and cranny for the little known facts. Gather so much information on your subject that your biggest problem will be deciding what to leave out! Don't become so impatient to begin earning money. First you must have something of genuine value to sell! The more complete your report, the more pride you'll have in it and the more you'll be able to charge for it when it is ready for sale. Read some of the lightly glossed over "How-To" articles you find in most magazines. See how much is left to the reader's imagination. Most of these give only enough information to whet your appetite. From there, if you really wish to know how to do it, you must start a minor research program on the subject anyway. Your reports must not be guilty of this type of glossing. Generalizations, the reader can pick up at any magazine stand for from 50 cents to a dollar - twenty-five.

HOW TO BECOME A RESEARCH EXPERT

The best place to start is usually your own neighborhood library or the bigger one downtown. Here you will ask the librarian to direct you to **THE READER'S GUIDE TO PERIODIC LITERATURE.** There is usually a separate table which contains these several volumes. At the same table you will also find **THE CUMULATIVE BOOK INDEX**, another set of reference volumes. The first will tell you, by subject matter, which magazines have published articles on your subject. Make notes of these ar go to the magazine racks and pick out those back issues. copy each article. Next, consult the Cumulative Book In **books** that have been published on your subject. Find th the shelves (or place an order for them if they are not in stock. The library will mail them to you when they are located).

One other reference book is **THE INDUSTRIAL INDEX** which lists, by subject matter, article titles that have been published in trade journals. Since these publications have a very limited readership, you will often find a gem of "how-to" information that readers of general readership magazines could never have found on their own, even by accident. The library will also have back copies of these journals and what you find there could be a veritable "gold mine" to you. Armed with the knowledge of only these three reference works you are, already, on your way to becoming a research **expert!**

tap! tap! tap! tap! tap! tap! tap! tap! tap!

Now let us suppose that thorough searching here did not produce the exact information you were seeking . . . where to go next? Well, you might consider searching the classified sections of mail order publications. Often, you will find exactly the information you need here, for a small fee. Send for it.

Ask friends and acquaintances what they know about your subject. Sometimes they will surprise you.

Write to universities and colleges. Explain that you are a writer and need research help. Address your letters to the "library research department." They are usually most cooperative and will at least suggest books if they don't exactly do the full research job for you. Often they will send pamphlets on your subject.

Write to the **UNITED STATES GOVERNMENT PRINTING OFFICE, Washington, D.C. (Superintendent of Documents)** P.O. Box 1821. Zip code: 20402. Ask to be placed on the circular mailing list for receiving **"SELECTED U.S. GOVERNMENT PUBLICATIONS."** Each month you will receive a pamphlet containing titles of hundreds of new government publications on an infinite variety of subjects. Some are free; all are reasonably priced if not free.

One of the most important publishing houses a business researcher can contact is **Gale Research Co.**, Book Tow troit, Michigan 48226. One priceless 2-volume set of ref books is the *Encyclopedia of Business Information Sourc* copyrighted in 1970. Check with them to see if they have an updated edition on this. It is the most important book you or your library can own. Another great **Gale** book is their *Encyclopedia of Associations*. In it are listed over 16,000 American associations. Most publish a monthly journal of some kind. An enterprising writer could gather up all back issues and compile an anthology of the best of "- - - - - - " to sell back to the membership.

HAVE YOUR NAME PLACED ON MAILING LISTS OF:

H. W. WILSON CO., 950 University Ave., N.Y.C., N.Y., 10452
PUBLISHER'S WEEKLY, 1180 Av O' Americas, NYC 10036. (R.R. BOWKER)
AB BOOKMAN'S YEARBOOK, Box 1100, Newark, N.J. 07101
SUNDAY Book Review, N.Y. TIMES, Times Square, N.Y.C. 10036.
PEOPLE'S ALMANAC, P.O. Box 49328, Los Angeles, CA 90049
STANDARD RATE & DATA Serv., 5201 Old Skokie Orch'd Rd., Skokie, IL 60076

There is a 158 page paper back book (presently $1.25) called *Reference Books: A Brief Guide* published by Enoch Pratt Free Library, 400 Cathedral St., Baltimore, MD 21201.

Another excellent work in paper back is *FINDING FACTS FAST* by Alden Todd. ($2.45) and published by William Morrow & Co., Inc., New York (1972). This book will tell you almost everything you need to know to become a research expert. (105 Madison Ave., New York, NY 10016)

Those who are serious researchers have an "insider's" technique when dealing with librarians. By presenting some form of convincing credentials, they are able to obtain a stack pass, which enables them to browse through the stacks in the library not normally open to the general public. Many books found here are not even catalogued by card number, and are old and very valuable sources of historical and other types of information.

It pays to have a certain number of inexpensive home reference volumes at your desk. One of the best is *The World Almanac,* on sale anually at your newstand. This is the standard American book of facts from which others were innaugurated. The others I refer to are: *Information Please Almanac* and *The New York Times Encyclopedic Almanac.* The strength of 1 *Almanac* lies in its excellent index, which includes bo subject headings and specific names.

T.O.W.E.R.S.

is an acronym for

"The Original Writer's Exchange Research Service"

How Towers Club, U.S.A. Was Born...

Are you interested in the subject of how ideas are born? Then you'll enjoy knowing what inspired this one. Many years ago I heard a minister tell a story in church. This story has had a profound effect on my life. It may have on yours too. Here it is:

A man died and found himself before the Pearly Gate, over which were printed the words "HEAVEN AND HELL". This certainly was not what he had been led to expect during his time in the body ... that Heaven and Hell would be located in the same place. He asked the gate keeper about it. "You'll understand at supper," was his reply. At supper time he was led to a huge dining hall. As he entered he was surprised to see it filled with people who had no elbows. They sat with arms stretched out straight before heaping plates of steaming food, but not being able to bend their arms they were unable to feed themselves. Each person at this table was gaunt and emaciated looking, apparently starving to "death" while seated at a banquet. "What's this?" the man asked of his guide. "Hell, Sir, but step this way." Through a portal they entered into an almost similar scene where a similar group, also unable to bend their arms sat at an equally abundant board. The immediately noticable difference was that this group was fat and rosy-cheeked, healthy and chattering gaily amongst themselves ... AS EACH TURNED AND FED HIS NEIGHBOR! This room was, of course, Heaven.

Those who join **TOWERS CLUB, USA** do so because they realize that there is no way on Earth they will ever be able to use every bit of information they come across in their everyday reading. The club offers them a system through which they can trade valuable information on a subject they don't plan to write about for valuable information on a subject they **do** plan to write on. It's a unique way of being able to practice the art of giving (which makes one feel wonderful) with the certainty that their giving will bring back the promised "ten-fold" fruits of "casting their bread upon the waters."

It costs only a postage stamp to send a newspaper clipping or a magazine article to someone who needs it more than you. In return you can expect to receive back an abundance of clippings on the subject nearest and dearest to your own interest. What could be simpler?

Currently, only 1 out of 3 who purchase this book join our club. Even if you are one who elects not to join, this book will amply cover everything you need to know to get a good rolling start at your first fortune, or at least a degree of financial independence few persons ever experience in a lifetime. I'm living proof it can be done . . . *and I didn't have this book to guide me!* **If I could have purchased this book in the beginning, I would have gladly paid a thousand dollars for it!**

THE MOLES & GOPHERS STORY

About the best place I've ever found to dig up little known trade secrets is by going to the logical person most likely to have run into the same problem in his line of work. The less that is known about your subject by the general public, the more valuable the the solution becomes to you as a researcher-writer. Let me give a good example from my own experience. In fact, **this story tells how I stumbled onto this formula.**

A few years back, my wife (Beverlee) and I left the city and bought a 100 acre farm in the hills of southern Oregon. We had just lost our only son in the Vietnam War and we needed a place to get away and lick our wounds. We named it Danhaven Farm (after our Danny) and it was the most beautiful farm in the world with five big shade trees around the old farm house and a babbling brook running right past the back porch.

We arrived in time to make a garden the first year. One problem we ran into was garden destruction by moles and gophers. It occurred to me that if I was having this problem, millions of other gardeners and farmers must be having the same one . . . yet, upon asking my more experienced neighbors, none seemed to have a solution.

"It's just something you'll have to learn to live with" was their collective, stoic reply. Well, I love a mystery . . . or a problem to which there is no seeming solution. Here was a "beaut!" So I started my first "How-To-Do-It" research project.

First, I went to my county agent . . . but he was dumber than the one on the old "Green Acres" T.V. show. Next I went to the library, but, not knowing what you know now about researching, I turned up very little of any value. The very fact that there was nothing of value in the library excited me even more because if no one had ever written a book on the subject it meant that when I **did** find the solution, I would have a **very** marketable piece of information. But, where was I to search if the farmers didn't know and the library didn't know? I decided to turn the question over to my subconscious mind. It could usually come up with an answer when everything else failed.

That night, before I dropped off to sleep, I used my conscious mind to do some deductive reasoning . . . "detective thinking", I call it. Who would be most likely to have this problem **but** also with enough motivation to have tried to solve it? I drifted off to sleep, still pondering. Next morning, I awoke with the solution, or at least a good clue. I awoke with the image of a beautifully cared for golf course before me. There was not a mole hill in sight. Of course! The greens keeper was the man I wanted to talk to!

STRAIGHT FROM THE HORSE'S MOUTH

During the next two days I visited every golf course in the area. I talked to every greens keeper. Each man had his own private method and he swore by it. Each was more than happy to talk about it when he learned I was a freelance writer preparing an article on the subject . . . especially when I snapped his picture with my 35 mm camera, his beloved greens behind him. He was proud of his work and wanted the world to know about it.

Back at the farm I set about putting these methods to the test. Sure enough, they seemed to work. As the summer wore on, I noticed fewer and fewer mole hills and at harvest time, my vegetables came through without harm. My garden was saved . . . but more important, I had stumbled onto the first step in my Writer's Utopia Formula . . . and I had the material for my first report!

It took less than a half hour to type up that first report. It was two pages of single-spaced copy on 8½ X 11 typing paper. I did my own crude drawings to illustrate it but they served the purpose. The report contained about 700 words. That's all . . . **but each word was a gem!** Each word served a purpose and there was no wasted verbiage. Anyone who read it would never have a mole problem in their garden again if they applied what they learned from it.

DOLLARS PER WORD, NOT PENNIES

To date I have realized more than $14,000.00 from the sale of that 700 word report. **That comes to $20.00 a word!** Not bad for an amateur writer . . . especially when you realize that the average trade publisher pays from 3 to 5 cents per word for the same kind of material **and once you sell it, it's his, not yours!** What's more, I fully expect to be selling that same article 20 years from now, the good Lord willing and the creek don't rise.

I'm going to tell you how I made that kind of money in the very next chapter . . . but first I want to ask you a question. If I offered to buy this book back at this point, before you turn the next page, how much would you sell it back for, if you knew you could never get a replacement? $25, $50, $100, $1,000? Would you sell it for any price? Check one answer below:

- [ ] I would sell it back right now for what I paid for it.
- [ ] I would sell it back right now for: $25.00
- [ ] $50.00
- [ ] $100.00
- [ ] $500.00
- [ ] $1,000.00
- [ ] It would cost you more than that!
- [ ] No deal! I bought it and I'm going to <u>KEEP IT</u>! I truly intend to retire early, while I can still enjoy it.

I realize you will only play the above game in your mind. Mentally, you have already checked one of the squares. If it was the first one, then the honorable thing to do would be to close this book right now and return it in unused condition and request your refund. To read further into the book and THEN request refund would be nothing short of stealing from the author, publisher.

I bargained with life for a penny
And life would pay no more
However I begged at evening,
When I counted my scanty store.

For life is a just employer;
He gives you what you ask,
But once you have set the wages,
Why, then you must bear the task.

I worked for a menial's hire,
Only to learn, dismayed,
That any wage I had asked of Life,
Life would have gladly paid.

Jessie B. Rittenhouse

PART TWO

Good! You've decided to stay with this purchase.

All the power you can ever use now exists and awaits your intelligent mastery!

O. K. - - THE REPORT IS RESEARCHED AND WRITTEN. TO WHOM DO WE SELL IT - - - AND HOW?

Without this formula, your first thought would be to follow along the well trodden path of most writers. . . typing up the perfectly spelled, punctuated, double-spaced manuscript, along with a letter to a publisher and a S.A.S.E. (Self Addressed Stamped Envelope), offering to sell all rights at his standard rate of pay. If you are a recognized, often-published writer you would sell it, maybe. You might realize as much as $150 for the article, but even then, you would have to wait months to get paid. They don't usually pay until the article is actually set in type and scheduled for publication. I once waited a full year to collect $40 for a 1500 word piece I sold to Fate Magazine. Such waits are not at all uncommon for the average freelance writer, selling to the trade publisher. A still worse fate is likely to happen to your manuscript. It **could** lay on the editor's desk or in his files for a year or so and then be returned **with a polite rejection slip!** It happens all the time. Is it any wonder only the very most dedicated writing aspirants stick to the task until they make a name for themselves?

I went to the trouble of learning the odds a neophyte book author has of being accepted by a trade publisher. Here they are: **Harper & Row, Publishers, Inc.,** one of the biggest, will get an average of 2600 books a year, unsolicited, over the transom. Of these, it may publish **ten.** In addition to the 2600 from unknowns there will be another 2000 from known and published authors. Of these, it will publish 230. The odds drop from **260 to 1,** for **unknowns** to, perhaps **9 to 1 for known authors.** American Review, the literary magazine is put out three times per year and they have 16,000 submitted manuscripts from which to choose.

THE WHOLE SHOW...

Needless to say, I didn't sell my 700 word "mole and gopher" report to a trade publisher! Neither will you with your own reports, if you follow my formula. Instead . . . YOU will become the publisher, editor, advertising account executive, art department-head, public relations specialist, sales manager and book retailer! - - - You will also be the copyright holder and the permanent recipient of all the profits from each and every report or book sold! I'm going to teach you enough, in the remainder of this book to become proficient in each of these areas!

AFTER YOUR REPORT IS WRITTEN, HERE'S WHAT TO DO.

Take your single-spaced, typewritten report to your local "Quick-Print Shop" and have at least 200 copies run off. (At present, (1974) in my home town, my printer charges me $7.80 for 200 sheets, printed on both sides). Prices will vary slightly from area to area but let's take that figure as a working average. Even if your report requires three sheets you have only invested $23.40. That's eleven and a half cents per package. Now, suppose you could sell all 200 at $3.00 each? That's $600 gross or $576.60 net profit, isn't it? Well, almost anyway. There is still the salesman's commission you must pay. If you are going to be the author and publisher you won't have much time to go out on the street and start selling your merchandise . . . or will you? Perhaps there's a better way to sell without all that fuss. Perhaps you can be the salesman after all . . . *without ever leaving home!*

Let's go back to my farming days . . . to the time when I had completed my "moles & gophers" report. That same day I had to run to town to pick up some grain at the feed store. While waiting for a clerk, I picked up a magazine and started idly thumbing through it. It happens it was "The Oregon Farmer-Stockman", a slick, multi-color production directed at, who else, farmers. Toward the back I noticed a classified section and a box appeal offering to accept ads at 12 cents per word. **CLICK!!! It all fell into place.** Here was a way to sell my "How to eliminate moles from your garden" report without ever giving up the copyrights to it. It certainly seemed worth a try.

I went directly home and composed a 14 word ad. It read: "ELIMINATE MOLES, GOPHERS quickly, easily, inexpensively! Guaranteed method. $2.00, Danhaven Farms" and my address. Simple arithmetic told me it would only cost $1.68 to put my message before several thousand farm families one time. The paper was a bi-weekly which meant I could buy the ad for $3.36 per month and have two chances a month to make sales. Although I wasn't exactly "flush" at that time, I decided I could not afford NOT to try it at that price. In fact, luckily for me, I made another important, critical decision. I decided to send $33.60 to pay for 10 consecutive insertions.

Well, as the man says, "You pays your money and you takes your chances." And for a while, there, I was sure my "pipe dream" had gone up in smoke. The first month I only took in $8.00. Four sales! It didn't look as though I was going to give Howard Hughes a run for the title of "richest man in the world" at this rate. But then, during the 10th to 12th weeks the flood gates broke loose and the $2.00 checks began pouring in. The lesson I learned there, at least with farm folk, is that they have to grow used to seeing your ad before they will venture with their money. The longer that ad ran, the more the percentage of replies continued to build. That ad is still running in that same paper to this day and I can't begin to count the money I've made from just that one publication. The rest of the story is elementary. Once I had proved that my selling method would work, I started expanding my advertising to more and more farm and gardening magazines. By winter I had raised my price from $2 to $3. There was no appreciable difference in the percentage of replies per dollar spent on advertising. But I never again grew discouraged if my ads didn't catch fire immediately. I knew they must age.

In the first year, I had a few buyers ask for refunds but as I continued to add more and more copy and drawings to my reports as I had more printed, the refund requests dropped to almost zero. Today I rarely get one.

I figure it has cost me approximately $2,500 in advertising to earn that $14,000 I spoke of, on this one report. That's $11,500 profit over a period of eight years for an article it took me **less than 2 days to research and a half hour to write**!

DIRECT RESPONSE SELLING

Now you know how you can become your own salesman. You do it through mail order, or as it has more recently been called, **DIRECT RESPONSE ADVERTISING AND SELLING.**

Let me clear up a common misconception before we go any further. Many folks think of MAIL ORDER as a business. **It is not!** It is a **way of doing business**. There's a big difference. It has been claimed that anything that is saleable can be sold via the mails . . **even real estate!**

You and I have chosen to sell *paper*. Our product is the printed word on paper. It's a simple commodity to stock and an easy product to deliver, once the order has been received. Thousands of enterprising persons have started building impressive fortunes from the privacy of a spare bedroom, basement or garage this way.

The name for a person who conducts a business such as this is *entrepreneur:* one who organizes, manages and assumes the risks of a business or enterprise. (Webster).

So, essentially then, to make the kind of money I have talked about in this formula, you must become a specialist in **three separate phases of business endeavor: (1) a research expert; (2) a master copywriter** (of simple, easy-to-understand language); and **(3) a mail order entrepreneur, willing to take the financial risks necessary to success.** If you can only afford to risk a few dollars in the beginning, then you may only make $1500 gross in the first year (assuming you have a good ad and a good product!) If, on the other hand, you are able and willing to invest several thousands of dollars in printing and advertising and postage, you could well be on your way to becoming an over-night tycoon in the field of **direct response.** As my old "Pappy" used to say at the poker table when he was holding a good hand - - "Come on boys, the more you put in, the more you take out." But there is always the word *risk* to be considered! In the entire history of man, there has never been a new business begun without an element of risk attached. Every new business venture involves at least a bit of **gambling** and **speculation.** You can win - - and you can also lose! A good example comes to mind. Recently, a new **TOWERS Club** member wrote that she had invested $168.75 in American Home Magazine on a classified ad to sell her 40 page report on "How to Expand Your Personality." The ad read as follows: **REVEAL THE MAGIC OF YOU - - Expand Your Personality. Secure happiness, sufficient money, lasting friendships. 40 page, power-packed instructions. Mail $5.00 (guaranteed)** . . . etc).

Had she consulted me first, she could have saved all that lost money (because she did not receive one single order). I would have advised her to re-write the ad, for one thing (or done it for her) but most important, I would have pointed out that the people who read the "Homes & Garden" magazines already have plenty of friends, plenty of money, security and (perhaps) even happiness. Her market would have been in the "Romance-Confession" magazines and the "teen-age" magazines. These people have still not arrived. They will buy instructions on how to be more popular, have more friends, make more money, etc. (Remember when you were sixteen, how unsure of yourself you were? Well, nothing has changed.)

The lady who wrote this report is an exceptionally gifted and intelligent person . . . and yet, she let her enthusiasm precede prudence. She forgot to use the common sense I told you was necessary to make a go of this or any other business. I have since advised her, but it is too early, at this writing to report on any new results. Sorry. (After that big disappointment she **did** see the value of joining our TOWERS Club, and she did so.)

In telling that story, I hope I have made my point very clear. You can win big . . . or you can lose money and become very discouraged.

I once saw a "Today's Chuckle" in the paper that went - - "If at first you don't succeed - - - you're running about average." For most people, I suppose that saying does apply - - - **but for you, if you are really digesting everything I write here, it should not apply at all! The chances of success on your very first try should be 95% or better!**

Needless to say, this book should be kept as your reference Bible!

How do you know, deep down inside, that you have written a winning report AND a winning ad? It's like falling in love. When it happens **YOU'LL KNOW IT!** If you've written the ad in such a manner that you are **certain YOU would send money for it**, it's a winner. **When you have written a report you would not be willing to sell back to the one who sold it to you, for twice the price you paid for it . . . you have written a winning report!** Until you have met those two requirements, go very easy on any advertising you buy for testing purposes.

TESTING YOUR ADS

Some of the old pro's test their ads in local newspapers, first. The reasons are multiple. First, you get immediate results data. You don't have to wait months to find out if you have a winner. Second, you get a local rate when advertising in a newspaper where you live. It's always less than they charge out-of-state advertisers. Third, it's easier to say "charge it" over the phone when you are dealing with your home town newspaper.

The next plateau, when buying national magazine advertising is to deal first with the "short term closing dates." This means you can order your ad by the 10th of August and it will appear in the October issue which comes out around the 15th of September By September 30th, you should have a sampling of how we ad pulled . . . in time to know if you want to repeat your order in the November issue. (Most Opportunity mags come under this "short term" heading). You get about 8 days of testing here.

With the more sophisticated magazines, you have no chance to test this way, since there is usually a two to three month wait between the time you pay for the ad and the time it actually hits the stands or is mailed out to subscribers. If your ad is a success, say in October, the earliest you can repeat would be February, unless you ordered consecutive insertions ahead of time. That's a gamble on an un-tested ad and a "no-no."

This advice applies particularly to expensive space ads with a coupon and an appeal for money. They can be very costly, or very inexpensive, depending on a myriad of variables. As of January 25, 1977, National Enquirer wanted $11,950 for a full page ad and $4.60 per word in a classified ad. Those numbers can make your eyes water a little bit when you're trying to work up the courage to write out a check for advance payment for an ad . . . especially if it is an ad you have not tested yet. But, on the other hand, if the ad has already been placed in a similar tabloid and at least returned the cost of the ad plus postage to mail out the orders, most old pros would not hesitate to run it again at the higher rates demanded by the leading tabloid. Once an ad is tested and has proved it can bring in even a slight profit, it is usually safe to roll out with the ad, during the peak months of the year; at least - (January through March and August through November).

THE PSYCHOLOGY OF SELLING BY MAIL

I could write several books on the subject of "what makes people buy?" but why should I? It's already been done by too many other qualified experts. The simple essence of the matter of selling and buying is that **if you tell enough people about your product or service, a certain percentage of them are going to buy on the spot!** You could be the village idiot selling puppy dog tails, but if you made your appeal enough times to enough people, you could exist off the profits from your sales. Starting from lowly premise, the only three factors in determining how living you'll make are: **how strong is the emotional appeal to the prospect; how fair is the price you are asking, and people are you going to present offers to buy to each**

That may be an over-simplification, and I'm sure it is, but the fact remains, these are the **three most important factors** in becoming a successful salesman **of anything**!

Willy, the protagonist of our little display ad exemplifies the average specialty salesman out in the field, trying to see enough people so that he can present his sales talk enough times to make enough sales to support himself and his family. Believe me, I speak from experience when I say that kind of selling ages a person far beyond his years. If every sales call resulted in a sale, then it wouldn't be so wearying, but those four turn-downs (on the average) for every sale grind a sales person into salt and sand in a few short years. Many of my readers have lived through this and are saying "**Amen**" to those words. Even worse is the aspect of having to travel and be away from home and hearth, family and fare for days or weeks at a time. It's a thrill for the first month and a drag for the rest of your sales career!

Now the beauty of selling by mail is just this: although your ratio of sales to presentations drops out of sight, you never again have to personally experience a turn-down. You only hear from the ones who read your sales message and decide to send **money**!

You can still become "an old friend" to your prospects. You do it by continuing to run your ads constantly in the same media. You can still strive to raise your ratio of **closes** by constantly improving your sales message. But once you have an ad that is doing the job "swimingly" leave it alone, sit back and let it be your commissioned salesman while you bask at poolside!

In selling by mail, you are only limited by the amount of money you are able and willing to risk on your own ad copy and the variety of media you are willing to risk it in!

As for learning the art of salesmanship – I once wrote a course in it that became nationally famous and sold for over $1,000. But, in a nutshell, all I told my students was this: ***Develop the principles contained in the Biblical tenet of The Golden Rule until they become an integral and dominating factor in your psychological make-up. When giving more than is expected of you becomes habitual - - relax and start concentrating on the*** *ness* of accepting a fair amount of money for the goods or *services* you are providing to your customers. There can be no *sin* in receiving just compensation for services rendered. Too *many* of the naturally kind people I have met, were also hung up on a misunderstanding of the Christian ethic. They failed to realize that it is God's will that we all live in abundance!

TWO METHODS OF MAIL ORDER ADVERTISING

1. Direct Mail. Don't confuse this term with "mail order". By "direct Mail," we mean the process of renting mailing lists (or building your own) and then mailing your sales letter to those names via third class mail. Such a postal permit costs $30. per year, renewable each January first. 3rd class allows you to mail in quantities of 300 pieces or more at a time at a reduced rate, or 50 pounds or 200 pieces of identical third-class bulk mail. With the third class bulk rate you usually save about 40% of the cost of first class rates. Write the Post Master General, Washington, D.C. for the government pamphlet titled "MAILING PERMITS."

2. Magazine, newspaper or radio - T.V. advertising. This method is further broken down into two separate methods: classified or display advertising (in printed publications). Those who start with classified ads only, usually graduate to larger and larger ads called "space" or "display" ads. These usually have some form of art work along with the copy and are a lot more successful in pulling power, of course. They also cost a lot more but are not necessarily "more expensive". It all depends on the response. In selling reports, we seldom get into radio advertising, or T.V.

Tom Hall, of Hong Kong advises his students to use only the **Direct Mail system.** It has been successful for him and he has become a very wealthy man selling reports this way.

On the other hand, Joe Karbo advises the direct response advertising method in magazines and newspapers. He has become a millionaire with this method. You've seen his "LAZY MAN'S WAY TO RICHES" ads in hundreds of publications. Strangely enough, he wrote that classic ad before he wrote the book. He was telling me about it when I visited him at his $30,000 summer cabin at Lake Cushman in August of 1976.

"Joe, how did you come to write your *'Lazy Man's'* book?" I asked, as we lunched on delicious smoked salmon and cold beer.

"Believe it or not, Jerry, I wrote the ad before I wrote the book. We used to have a much smaller cabin here at the lake. One night I was having trouble sleeping, so I got up and went to my typewriter at the kitchen table. Within 2 hours, I had written the ad I'm still running. When I got back to California, I tested its pulling power in our local paper. It worked fine. After that, it only took a few days to knock out the book and have it printed at a local print shop. Meanwhile, I rolled-out with the ad in national magazines and the rest is history."

And history it is. As close as I can figure, he has sold over **500,000** of those books at $10 . . . and each one costs him less than fifty cents. No big publisher or distributor is creaming the usual 90% of the gross. Karbo pays for his own ads and reaps **ALL the profits**!

JOE & BETTY KARBO at the cabin ... leaning on the "green monster."

Today (1977), Joe and Betty Karbo vacation several months of the year. They own a condominium apartment on the beach in Hawaii where they spend the spring and early summer. Then in June, usually, they fly to the cabin in the Olympic Mountains of Washington State where most of their life-long friends live, many of whom own neighboring cabins. Sometime in August, the Karbo's get in about 3 weeks of salmon fishing at La Push Indian Reservation and Resort at the ocean. Then they loaf the rest of the summer away sailing on the lake or taking side trips around Washington State or up into Canada. After Labor Day, they return to that $100,000 house in Huntington Beach (Which is probably worth 4 times that amount by now), where Joe acts in local theater groups and in his spare time, directs his well staffed offices and places all his ads for the coming year. He no longer drives a Cadillac. It's a green Rolls Royce with the letters "KARBO" on the license plate.

What's the secret to his success? There are lots of them ... but in a nutshell ... he is a good writer, a smart business man, and he's not afraid to gamble his dollars on his own talent. In other words, he's the classic example of an entrepreneur. He knows how to use his own creative imagination. He creates ORIGINAL ideas, instead of copying what others have done, and he puts his money where his head is. Maybe it helps to have a wife named Betty - - - -

Not long ago, I had the pleasure of sharing a delicious Chinese dinner in Seattle with my friends, Hubert and **Betty** Simon of Yonkers, New York. Hubert has been in the business of selling his own How-To reports for more than 25 years, by mail order and magazine ads. They maintain a large staff in their office, own several printing machines and produce 4 or more monthly newsletters, in addition to selling reports. Like the Karbos, they are seldom there anymore. They spend most of their time ocean-hopping by jet, to Europe. They especially love England, and go there as many as five times a year. Yes, they have it locked, now, but in the beginning, Hube was just out of the service, a young man with no job, a pregnant wife and mountains of bills. Instead of sitting around moping, he rented a small office in New York (on credit) and started sending out letters. A few of them got action and he was off and running with his first mail order idea. Many fine folios have steamed out of his typewriter since then and Hubert and Betty Simon have never known what it is to be overdrawn at the bank since.

As a student at UCLA, handsome young Dan Martino built a reputation for "having a way with the ladies." Friends were always asking his advice on the subject. He decided to cash in on this "talent," so he wrote a 4-book course on the subject and dropped out of school to become his own publisher/marketer. At last report, he had signed up over 10,000 men in his *"Dan Martino School For Men"* at $35 apiece. And this was only in 1976. Let's keep an eye out for this new entrepreneur in years to come !

Twenty years ago, Arthur Frommer was a newly discharged G.I. with a law degree. But he never got around to hanging out his Law shingle. He got interested in writing a book instead. It was titled *"Europe on $5 A Day."* It covered all the little known secrets he had picked up in the Service overseas; tips on how to travel for next to nothing. It never occurred to him to submit it to a trade publisher. He had it typeset and printed and started selling it himself. Today he has a string of similar books, only now it's "On $10 A Day", and he also owns a string of hotels all over the world. He's another millionaire, because he published his own brain children !

Miss Lanie Dills, 32, of Nashville, TN was a traveling saleslady for the 3-M Company when the CB-Radio boom hit. She bought one and then made a quick research study on "CB talk" so she could understand what those crazy truckers were talking about. Then she put it all into a super little book called *"The Official CB Slanguage/Language Dictionary."* Every smart publisher in N.Y. told her to forget it ... so she went to her local banker, Clarence Reynolds of Nashville's Commerce Union Bank, and talked him into a $10,000 loan for 90-days. He claims it was the riskiest loan he ever made, but she paid it back with only one extension. The book sold 80,000 copies under her own efforts, and then she turned it over to a marketing firm in New York and it hit the New York Times best-seller list and stayed there from May to September, 1976. They sold 516,000 copies at $2.95 and Miss Dills banked $464,000 in her own little checking and savings account. Those "smart" New York publishers are still scratching their heads and spitting.

One day in April, 1975, Gary Dahl was spending a leisurely afternoon in the *Sirloin & Grog,* a friendly neighborhood bar just around the corner from his little rented cottage, engaged in his favorite pastime ... drinking good scotch whiskey and entertaining his fellow patrons with his droll wit. Most advertising men do this, and Dahl is an advertising man. That day, he started bragging about his "pet rock", off the top of his head, and the more he joked, the funnier his concept became. That was the birth of an idea which was to make him close to a million dollars before Christmas. He decided to put plain old river rocks in boxes, along with a little booklet he would write on "The Care And Feeding Of Your Pet Rock." It was a put-on towards those people who constantly bore you to tears with tales about their Poodle or cat. The marketing story of Pet Rocks is common knowledge now, but how many of us really gave enough credit to the gimmick that made the rocks into a whirl-wind fad? It wasn't the rocks, ... it was the funny little book that went with them!

By Christmas of 1975 Dahl had made enough money to buy a huge mansion with a swimming pool, and a cocktail lounge of his own, which he still operates in Los Gatos, California, while a competent staff still operates his *"Rock Bottom Productions"* from another office down the street. No, he did not promote the rocks through a mail order campaign. Instead, he sold them through retail outlets. First he talked a few local stores around home into trying them as a gag. A few little publicity blurbs in the local papers engineered by the media-savy advertising man and suddenly the stores couldn't keep enough Pet Rocks in stock to satisfy the wildly demanding public. With this bonanza at the local level, it didn't take Gary Dahl long to bring the delightful story of Pet Rocks to the national media through news releases to several of the newswire services. Once the story broke nationally, Dahl didn't need to ask department store buyers to place orders. They were fighting each other to get in line.

NEWSLETTER PUBLISHING CAN BE PROFITABLE TOO !

It's risky business to pay compliments to any businessman before he is dead, I know ... and yet, I feel reasonably safe in mentioning just a few other mail order publishers who have become well-to-do in this business, and who seem to give excellent value for the money they charge. I won't give their address, for fear you might suspect I had been paid to plug them. (I have not). But, if you see their ads, you might feel a little safer in sending them your money, after seeing their names here:

John Chase Revel, (Insider Reports) - Santa Monica, CA
Thad Stevenson, (Opportunity Knocks) - Santa Rosa, CA
Jerry Buchanan, (TOWERS Club, USA N/L) - Vancouver, WA
J. W. Straw, (Business Opportunities Digest N/L) - Clarksville, TN.
David E. Reeves, (Car Owners of America) Menlo Park, CA
Howard Penn Hudson (Newsletter on N/L's), Rhinebeck, N.Y.
Herb Ahrend, (Copy Cornucopia N/L) - New York City
B. L. Mellinger, (World Trade Business) - Woodland Hills, CA
G.W. Haylings, (Money-Making Communique) Carlsbad, CA
G. D. Hafely, Jr., (CA$H-CO N/L), Brooksville, FLA

Each of the above are monthly newsletter publishers. I have spent my own money to subscribe to each, and can report satisfaction and full value received. Now, if you are a prominent newsletter publisher, and would like to put me on your complimentary mailing list for say six months, I may be able to list your publication and name here, next time we revise WUFR.

What these people have done, you can too -- with a little imagination !

NOTE: The good newsletter of today, is usually the good magazine of tomorrow !

WHO'S MAKING THE MOST MONEY ?

Of all the mail order entrepreneurs who have become fabulously wealthy selling "words", few are so wealthy as those who took the religious approach. I don't mean to imply they were false religionists, in it only for the money and the tax breaks. Many of these men and women were totally sincere in their belief and in their desire to help their fellow men. BUT, many were not too!!!

In the eyes of our Federal laws, every American is free to teach or believe in the religion of his choice, no matter how far-out or ridiculous it may seem to conventional society. You are allowed, by the words of the First Amendment, to worship nails or snails or puppy-dog tails; sugar or spice or everything nice. Just in case you were asleep when they taught this in high school U.S. history class, here is a brief review lesson:

A SHORT U. S. HISTORY LESSON

On December 15th, 1791, the Congress of the United States added the first ten original amendments to our Constitution. Number one was worded as follows:

Congress shall make no law respecting an establishment of religion, or prohibiting the free exercise thereof; or abridging the freedom of speech, or of the press; or the right of the people peaceably to assemble, and to petition the Government for a redress of grievances.

What makes this legal loophole even more appealing to the profit-minded religionist is that churches are allegedly "non-profit" institutions, which means they are tax exempt. There is no law though, that limits the amount of salaries the "board" can vote for the "staff" which might consist of the minister, his wife, his mother-in-law and his five children. What's more, there are no academic legal requirements on any law books. You do not need a fancy college of divinity sheepskin. It's common knowledge in the Bible tent brigade that many of the most famous evangelists just "up and started preaching one day."

BECOME A MINISTER
(Men & Women)

Be ordained in the UNIVERSAL LIFE CHURCH. Legally perform marriages and all other religious ceremonies. Send to: UNIVERSAL LIFE CHURCH, 1023 N. Vermont Ave., Dept. NS L.A., Ca. 90029 213-666-1160. Your ministerial credential is sent by return mail. A tax deductible donation to cover our expenses will be appreciated.

At left is a typical Universal Life Church ad (clipped from National Star, Mar 15, 1977). Yes, my Bible-scholar friends, I DID notice the "666" digits in phone number, and yes, I DID think about Revelations 13: 17 - 18. Calling the number every day for a week - - only brought the same recorded message -- to call Avalon 98 on Catalina Island, or call the "666" number back after noon on Tuesday. Catalina didn't answer, and Tuesday came and went and the same message remained on the answering machine. 3/18/77.

In recent years, new churches and ministers have been springing up out of the weeds like dandelions on a spring day. The IRS is not at all happy about it, but their hands are tied. By conservative estimate, about **three million new churches and ministers** have emerged out of nowhere in the past decade, and now one enterprising mail order genius is selling a book on *"RELIGION CAN MAKE YOU RICH! - - Financially As Well As Spiritually."* It is a set of three books, actually, for which the fellow asks you to send him a $20 free will offering to defray costs and help his church. Operator's name appears in ad, out of a city in New Jersey; a pretty moxie guy in mail order. He is always on to the latest mail order gimmick before the rest of the pack, it seems. Only he is usually copying somebody else who has pioneered the way first. This time, he is copying a man in California named Kirby Hensley. A most interesting personality, indeed. You may have seen him being interviewed by Mike Wallace on the television show "60-Minutes" in the winter of '76-

'77. Hensley is a one-time preacher who turned atheist and then started the *Universal Life Church,* a mail order scheme to sell official ordainments. Anybody with a spare twenty dollar bill can, by sending it to Hensley, become a marrying, burying, baby-Christenin', Bible-thumpin', circuit-stumpin.' Sunday-go-to-meeting, genuine minister in the *ULC.* When the Internal Revenue Service decided to take old tongue-chewing Reverend Hensley to court over his activities, he fooled them by carrying the battle right to them ... and winning his case. The decision handed down by Federal District Court Judge Batten, has since become a landmark decision. Here it is, verbatim :

FEDERAL JUDGE BATTEN'S EARTH SHAKING DECISION IN THE UNIVERSAL LIFE CHURCH TRIAL.

"Neither this Court, nor any branch of this Government will consider the merits or fallacies of a religion. Nor will the Court compare the beliefs, dogmas and practices of a newly organized religion with those of an older, more established religion. Nor will the Court praise or condemn a religion, however excellent or fantastical or preposterous it may seem. Were the Court to do so, it would impinge upon the guarantees of the First Amendment."

And so as we go to press with this latest revision, Rev. Hensley in Los Angeles and the other fellow in New Jersey, with similar sounding names on their respective "churches" continue to sell official sanction to marry and bury at $20 a crack. Strangely enough, the guy in New Jersey, whose city we'll let you discover for yourself, but whose street address is "4 Cherry St.", gives us cause to pause and snicker a little. It seems that at that very same address, for only $19.95, you can buy a book entitled - - *"Why S. O. B. 's Succeed and Nice Guys Fail in a Small Business."* An so you see, my friends, for $20, give or take a nickel, you can become either a Bible-thumpin' heathen-chaser, or a certified Son Of A Bitch. Take your choice and pay your money.

It's not my intention, in these brief few pages to pass judgment on any man or woman who has chosen the religious path as a "calling." Long before America was born, we had such men as John Wesley and John Calvin starting churches. Then as the twentieth century dawned with renewed religious enlightenment we had such men as Dwight L. Moody, Billy Sunday and Father Dyer stumping the back woods with tent-meeting revivals and one great agnostic, Col. Robert Greene Ingersoll stumping right behind them, and pointing out the fallacies of their words and (what he claimed were) their crooked, twisted scruples. He was a mighty rhetorician and his logic was formidable, but by then, the revivalists had their spurs dug in far too deeply into the American psyche. Religion was here to stay. And the longer it stayed, the more those traveling evangelists seemed to learn their trade. The more they seemed to understand about salesmanship, mass hypnotism, modern psychology and mob hysteria. And the more they learned, the more money they found in their collecttion plates after every meeting. Religion became big business, and we met the likes of Aimee Semple Mc Pherson, Billy Sunday, Father Divine, C. E. Coughlin, Carl Mc Intire, Billy James Hargis, Reverend Ike, Marjoe Gortner and Rev. Sun Myung Moon. Herbert W. Armstrong was ordained "by Jesus, Himself." That was in 1931, in Eugene, Oregon, when Armstrong, an out-of-work advertising man needed a better way to support his family. Today, his World Wide Church of God takes in $50 million a year in donations, and son Garner Ted is the golden-boy of the air waves and mail order business, as his father used to be.

I have presented this portion of WUFR because I feel it has a valid place in this book. How you readers use the ideas here will be up to you. One man in Fresno, California who calls himself, simply, "Brother Al" started a mail order church in 1974 and went hot and heavy with the 2 column, six inch ads for about a year. Now that he has his mailing list, he just sits back and milks it for all the traffic will bear. Is that a "church" ... or a license to steal? I'm on his mailing list ... so I know his scam.

Pilate saith unto him, What is truth? And when he had said this, he went out again unto the Jews, and saith unto them, I find in him no fault at all. JOHN 18:38

YOUR OWN BEST WRITING STYLE

The following article originally appeared in Reader's Digest in August, 1973, and is reproduced here with permission of the publisher. We recommend that you purchase a copy of the entire book, *"Say What You Mean"* by Rudolph Flesch, ($5.95), by Harper & Row, Inc., 10 E. 53rd St., N.Y.C. 10022.

WRITE THE WAY YOU TALK

Try the "open shirt and blue jeans" style of writing—you'll be more effective

RUDOLF FLESCH
Author of "How to Write, Speak and Think More Effectively," etc.

NINETY-NINE percent of the people who come to my writing classes were born nonwriters and have stayed that way all their lives. For them, writing has always been an unpleasant chore; answering a simple letter looms ahead like a visit to the dentist. But they have to do a certain amount of writing in their careers. And knowing their writing was poor, they decided to do something about it.

No doubt when you think about improving your writing, you think of grammar, rhetoric, composition, —all those dull things you learned year after year in school. But most likely, these things are not your problem. You probably have a pretty good grip on these essentials. What you need is instruction in the basic principles of professional writing.

Why professional writing? Because you now write as you did in school, unconsciously trying to please the teacher by following the rules of "English composition." You're not really writing a letter to the addressee, or a report for your vice president. The pros—magazine writers, newspapermen, novelists, people who write for a living—learned long ago that they must use "spoken" English and avoid "written" English like the plague.

Talk on paper. The secret to more effective writing is simple: *talk* to your reader. Pretend the person who'll read your letter or report is sitting across from you, or that you are on the phone with him. Be informal. Relax. Talk in your ordinary voice, your ordinary manner, vocabulary, accent and expression. You

"SAY WHAT YOU MEAN," COPYRIGHT © 1972 BY RUDOLF FLESCH, IS PUBLISHED AT $5.95
BY HARPER & ROW, PUBLISHERS, INC., 10 E. 53 ST., NEW YORK, N.Y. 10022

Condensed from "SAY WHAT YOU MEAN"

WRITE THE WAY YOU TALK

wouldn't say "Please be advised," or "We wish to inform you." Instead, something like, "You see, it's like this," or "Let me explain this." One helpful trick is to imagine yourself talking to your reader across a table at lunch. Punctuate your sentences, in your mind, with a bite from a sandwich. Intersperse your thoughts with an occasional "you know," or the person's name.

So talk—talk on paper. Go over what you've written. Does it look and sound like talk? If not, change it until it does.

Use contractions freely. There's nothing more important for improving your writing style. Use of *don't* and *it's* and *haven't* and *there's* is the No. 1 style device of modern professional writing. Once you've learned this basic trick, you can start producing prose that will be clear, informal and effective.

Take the standard opening phrase: "Enclosed please find." What's a better way of saying that? Simply, "Here's"!*

Leave out the word "that" whenever possible. You can often omit it without changing the meaning at all. Take this sentence: "We suggest that you send us your passbook once a year." Now strike out *that.* Isn't this better and smoother? Again, this is something we do all the time in speaking.

And while you're crossing out *thats,* also go on a *which* hunt. For some reason people think *which* is a more elegant pronoun. Wrong. Usually you can replace *which* by *that,* or leave it out altogether—and you'll get a better, more fluent, more "spoken" sentence.

Use direct questions. A conversation is not one-sided. One person speaks, then the other interrupts, often with a question, like "Really?" or "Then what?" A conversation without questions is almost inconceivable. So use a question whenever there's an opportunity, and your writing will sound more like talk.

You don't have to go out of your way to do this. Look at what you write and you'll find indirect questions—beginning with *whether*—all over the place. "Please determine whether payment against these receipts will be in order." No good. Make it: "Can we pay against these receipts? Please find out and let us know."

Or take another sentence: "Your questions and comments are invited." Again, this is really a question: "Do you have any questions or comments? If so, please let us know." There's nothing like a direct question to get some feedback.

Use personal pronouns. A speaker uses *I, we* and *you* incessantly—they're part of the give-and-take of conversation. Everybody, it seems, who writes for a company or organization clings desperately to the passive voice and avoids taking the slightest responsibility. He doesn't say *we,* never says *I,* and he even avoids using the straightforward

---

*Though most of my examples are taken from business correspondence, the principles apply to *all* types of writing.

you. So we find phrases like "It is assumed..." "it will be seen..." "it is recommended...." Or sentences like: "An investigation is being made and upon its completion a report will be furnished you." Instead, write, "We've made an investigation and we'll furnish you a report."

Normally, when writing for an organization, there isn't too much opportunity to say "I." But do use "I" whenever you express feelings and thoughts that are your own. Often it's better to say "I'm sorry," or "I'm pleased," than "we're sorry" or "we're pleased." And call the addressee *you*. The idea is to make your writing as personal as possible.

It's all right to put prepositions at the end. For 50 years, English-language experts have unanimously insisted that a preposition at the end is fine and dandy. H. W. Fowler, in *A Dictionary of Modern English Usage*, 1926, defends it enthusiastically and cites examples from Shakespeare and the Bible to Thackeray and Kipling. Yet schoolteachers still tell pupils they should never commit such a wicked crime.

Put the preposition at the end whenever it sounds right to do so. Instead of "The claimant is not entitled to the benefits for which he applied," write "The claimant isn't entitled to the benefits he applied for." Remember, grammatical superstitions are something to get rid of.

Spill the beans. There's a natural tendency in all of us to begin at the beginning and go on to the end. When you write a letter, it's the easiest way to organize your material. The trouble is, it's hard on the reader. He has a problem, or a question, and wants to know whether the answer is yes or no. If he has to wait until you're willing to tell him, his impatience and subconscious resentment will increase with every word. Rather than stumbling your way through some awkward introduction, start right in with the most important thing you want to get across. Plunge right in.

Re:...
Gentlemen:
   In reference to the above collection item, which you instructed us to hold at the disposal of the beneficiary, we wish to advise that Mr. Ling has not called on us, nor have we received any inquiries on his behalf.
   The above information is provided to you in the event you wish to give us any further instructions in the matter.

Cross out everything up to the words "Mr. Ling." Then the letter becomes (with a few other minor changes):

Re:...
Gentlemen:
   Mr. Ling hasn't called on us, nor have we had any inquiries on his behalf. Do you have any further instructions?

You see what this does? Once the unnecessary verbiage is cleared away, the letter becomes downright elegant.

Write short, snappy sentences. The ordinary reader can take in only

WRITE THE WAY YOU TALK

so many words before his eyes come to a brief rest at a period. If a sentence has more than 40 words, chances are he's been unable to take in the full meaning. So break those long sentences apart, 20 words at most. It's usually quite easy to see where one idea leaves off and another begins. Then try writing *really* short sentences every so often, and watch your letters and reports wake from their customary torpor.

Use short words. Long, pompous words are a curse, a curtain that comes between writer and reader. Here are some familiar sayings as they would appear in a business letter. "In the event that initially you fail to succeed, endeavor, endeavor again." "All is well that terminates well."

Everybody has his own pet pomposities. Banish them from your vocabulary. Replace *locate* with *find; prior to* with *before; sufficient* with *enough; in the event that* with *if.* After those simple substitutions, weed out such other words as *determine, facilitate* and *require* whenever they show up. You'll find that it's possible to live without them. And you'll learn to appreciate the joys of simple language.

Write for people. By far the most important thing is to give your letters just the right human touch. Express your natural feelings. If it's good news, say you're glad; if it's bad news, say you're sorry. Be as courteous, polite and interested as you'd be if the addressee sat in front of you. Some human being will read your letter and, consciously or unconsciously, be annoyed if it is cold, pleased if you're courteous and friendly.

A bank got a letter from a customer who'd moved from New York to Bermuda. He wrote to make new arrangements about his account. The bank's answer started: "We thank you for your letter advising us of your change of address." Now really! How stony and unfeeling can you get? I would at least have said something like "I noted your new address with envy."

You'll find there are rewards for improving your written work. This is the age of large organizations where it's easier to catch the eye of a superior by what you write than by what you say or do. Write the way I suggest and your stuff will stand out. Beyond the material rewards are more personal ones. When you write a particularly crisp, elegant paragraph, or a letter that conveys your thoughts clearly and simply, you'll feel a flow of creative achievement. Treasure it. It's something you've earned.

"HECK, I CAN'T SPEL VARY GUD"

If you are a good typist, speller and punctuator you are a very rare person! Most of the best-selling novelists and writers are not! Does that statement surprise you? Those who are proficient in these skills are the men and women who make only a fair living as secretaries, stenographers and professional typists. They are (Lord forgive me for saying it) the drones of the writing and publishing profession.

You can hire them for next to nothing, compared to the valuable services they provide to creative writers. If you doubt that, then go this minute to your nearest magazine stand and purchase a copy of the current *Writer's Digest Yearbook.* Somewhere near the back you will find a full double page with nothing but secretarial services advertisements. They are begging to do your tough work for you. The average charge? Maybe .45 cents a page for double-spaced, 8½ X 11 page with minor corrections included! What a shame those girls have never learned what you are learning! **They are starving to death with a loaf of bread under each arm!**

"BUT I CAN'T FIND THE TIME TO WRITE"

Before you protest you haven't enough time to become a prolific writer, let me . . . in the vernacular of our young . . . ***blow your mind*** with some astounding literary accomplishment facts from the *"Guinness Book of World Records."* (Another good reference source for information that will "punch-up" your copy).

Charles Hamilton, *alias* **Frank Richards,** the Englishman who created ***Billy Bunter*** used to average writing 80,000 words a week ! His lifetime output was at least 72 million words!

The Belgian writer. **Georges Simenon,** creator of ***Inspector Maigret,*** wrote a novel of 200 pages in 8 days. In April, 1973 he completed his 214th and last novel under his own name, of which 78 were about Inspector Maigret. He has also written **300 other novels under 19 other pen names** since 1919. These are published in 31 countries in 47 languages and have **sold more than 300,000,000 copies! (Three hundred million).**

From 1931 to 1973, the British novelist **John Creasey** (1908-73) wrote under his own name and 13 aliases, 564 books totaling **more than 40 million words.** He turned out 15 to 20 novels per year with a record of 22 one year. **He once wrote two books in a week with a half - day off to spare!**

From 1922 to July, 1972 authoress Ursula Bloom had 468 full-length books published, including the best sellers *The Ring Tree* (novel) and *The Rose of Norfolk* (non-fiction).

Erle Stanley Gardner (1889-1970) of *Perry Mason* fame dictated up to 10,000 words per day and worked with his staff on up to as many as seven novels simultaneously. His sales on 140 titles reached **170 million by the time he died!**

Walter Gibson, creator of the famous **The SHADOW** mysteries wrote 283 SHADOW novels (about 60,000 words each), a feat even more remarkable because during seven consecutive years (out of fifteen) he wrote one novel **every two weeks, on schedule!** (It's an interesting side note that Gibson, Mark Twain and several other famous authors claimed that they received their plots and inspirations through psychic forces they couldn't explain!)

If you claim you're **too young** to write, I'll point to **Janet Aitchison** who wrote a children's book when she was 5½ and had it published **when she was 6½ years old!**

If you claim to be **too old** . . . consider **Mrs. Alice Pollock** who had her latest novel published in 1971 when she was more than **102 years old.** (Born July 2nd, 1868). The book was *"My Victorian Youth"* and wouldn't we love to read that one?

It took man 5,000 + years before it was discovered it was possible for him to run the mile in under four minutes. Once it was done it became common for long distance milers to break the four-minute mile regularly. Now that you know what is possible in the field of writing, don't ever let me hear you say you can't turn out 700 words of good, finished copy per day!

Isaac Asimov, science-fiction genius is a one-man book-of-the-month club. He's written 76 in 76 months...179 books in 26 years. Turns out a non-fiction book in 70 hours.

"I wrote a book entitled *'How to Enjoy City Living'* and made enough to buy this place."

...E ART OF USING EMOTIONAL APPEAL

...u are just about ready to start your personal journey to ...R'S UTOPIA. I'm sure, by now, you can see the tremendous ...ossibilities in this way of writing for a fantastic income. No more will you ever experience the crushing dissapointment of opening an envelope to find a polite rejection slip. Never again will you wait month on agonizing month for a publisher to let you know what he thought of your manuscript. Never will you be in the frustrating position of not being able to submit your story to a likely publisher because it hasn't been returned from the last one yet. From now on, you should be able to sell everything you can write, over and over again, for as long as you live! **Not for pennies per word but for many, many dollars per word!**

If you eventually grow to the place where you have placed hundreds of ads for 8 or 9 years consecutively before you decide to retire and quit advertising, you will still be receiving money orders in the mail for years to come. Were you aware of that? Yes, your magazine ads will continue to work for you years after you **have retired to Florida or Hawaii or Mexico. Be sure and leave a forwarding address and take a supply of your reports to mail out.**

Here's another lesson in salesmanship ... a vital one! Every professional advertising copywriter and every professional salesman works from the basic premise that the buyer will not open up the purse until the seller rings the proper *emotional bell.* Every major buying decision any of us ever make is first triggered by a strong emotional appeal, under one of the 5 headings below:

1. SELF-PRESERVATION
2. FAMILY
3. ROMANCE
4. MONEY
5. RECOGNITION

Any other emotional area you can name can be fitted under one of these FIVE MAJOR areas of your emotional mechanism!

Keep these five major appeals always in your mind! When you ...picking a subject to research and write about, ask yourself : ...is subject lend itself to one of the **five major emotion-** ...ls? Will I be able to build a sales talk in my advertising or ...tter around this subject? How many of these five can I draw on when preparing my sales material?" **The more, the better!** You want something that will make your small classified ads **sing** and **bubble** and **dance!** You want something to excite the imagination of the reader; send his mind reeling off into space with visions of **pleasure, romance, travel, love, money, adventure, glory, fame, self-esteem, acceptance, security, riches** and whatever else you can think of!

WRITING AND PLACING CLASSIFIED ADS - - -
(More on writing classifieds, page 49)

Perhaps you are an old hand at writing and placing classified ads. Even so, don't skip this chapter. You still might pick up a few pointers.

Writing an ad is like writing a "formula sales pitch." Once you get the wording just right, you should never change it. **Benson Barrett** of Chicago, (Another mail order millionaire) has used the same wording in his small classified ads ever since I can remember. He simply says: *"Make money writing short paragraphs at home."* Just seven words tell his entire story. It's a masterpiece of brevity and it works for him. Adding even one word could add thousands of dollars a year to his advertising costs. Even though he places expensive full-page space ads in many magazines, he never gives up his little classified ads. You see them everywhere. They are the "bread & butter" of his advertising program.

David Magee of Kerrville, Texas is another "over-night" millionaire, by his own boast, who seldom runs a space ad over the size of one column, 3 inches, yet his classified ads are ubiquitous. Since he sells many different reports, his ad wording is not always the same. Let's look at one of his more common ones.

45

HOW & WHERE to get capital. Get loans, grants, cash. $500 to $2 million. Free information (and the address).

Do you see any wasted words? I do. In the first two lines he used the word *get* twice when once would have been sufficient, simply by using another comma. He also could have used *details* instead of *free information* and saved the expense of another word. The old school of advertising copy writing has long held that the word *free* is worth its weight in gold. That's for you to determine in your own ad testing. I've tried it both ways without much observable difference. If you haven't specified a dollar amount to be sent for *details,* the reader naturally must assume it is going to be *free.*

Details or *free details* is an advertiser's way of saying: "My sales story is too long to tell in this ad so I am going to send you an envelope containing a sales letter, a coupon, the price of my service and a postage paid return envelope to make it easier for you to order what I have to sell."

In most cases, a classified ad can't be expected to buy you much more than the name and current address of a slightly interested prospective buyer. My "Mole & gopher" ad is an exception to this rule. Classified ads can pull money directly, but they must **offer something unique** and be placed in a magazine specializing in the subject being offered. My "mole" ad runs only in farm and gardening magazines. General readership publications would have too many apartment dwellers who would not be interested and thus my advertising dollars would not return the necessary 3 to 1 mark-up. (More about pricing, pages 55 - 59.)

PUTTING A TITLE TO YOUR REPORT

"The Lazy Man's Way to Riches" and *"Out of the Rat Race and into the Chips"* are both titles of books. Well chosen titles, I hasten to add, because **each could be used as the wording for a complete classified ad wording. Each is used as a full page heading of a successful space ad.**

Each tells a complete and compelling story in the fewest possible words. After you have spent a few hours trying to compose the perfect **"one-liner"** for your classified ad, you will find that you have named your report as well. If buyers send money from the wording of such an ad, and you send them a book or manuscript with that title, they can't later complain that they did not get exactly what they sent for! No misrepresentation!

DELAYS IN FILLING MAIL ORDERS ILLEGAL NOW

Karbo and Emery (below) got away with running ads before the books were finished. This is no longer possible, since the FTC passed new and more stringent regulations in February, 1976. Writers ALWAYS misjudge how soon they will complete a book. Printers NEVER deliver jobs at time they promised they would.

Carla Emery of Kendrick, Idaho, a "back-to-the-land" enthusiast got the idea of writing an *"Old Fashioned Recipe Book"* using recipes from her grandmother's files. In her enthusiasm, she placed ads and was overwhelmed with the money response. In her spare time, she then began writing the book. Finally, 4 years and 3 babies later, her book was finished. By this time she had sold 1,300 copies "on the come." In the first month, alone, from ads in several magazines she received over 200 $3.50 orders. This was too good to be true, so she allowed the ads to continue to run. Meanwhile, she prepared a letter and a fabulous **Table of Contents** and mailed it to all her buyers, explaining that the book was still being written and that she would forward a **better product than they had paid for** if they would only be patient. It worked. At last report, she had sold over **46,000** copies at $12.95 PLUS starting a "Back To The Land" school on the 386-acre farm she bought with the profits. In August of 1975, a flood wiped the entire new campus out, so she's given up that idea. At last report, she had sold publishing rights to Bantam but retains rights to publish and market her mimeographed edition. Deals like Emery's and Karbo's, where the ads were run before the book was printed and made ready for delivery are no longer legal. New Postal laws require that you either deliver as advertised within 30 days or notify buyer of delay. If you can not deliver within the following 30 days, you must, by law, return the money without hesitation. In the first 30-day notice, you are required to offer money-back at that time, and allow buyer to decide whether to wait further or get money back.

ONCE YOUR SURE-FIRE AD IS WRITTEN, WHERE DO YOU PLACE IT AND HOW?

Your library should have at least one of the huge reference volumes used by professional advertising agencies. (1) Standard Rate & Data, (2) Ayer's, or (3) Ulrich's. If your library has none of these, ask them to order S.R. & Data from Skokie, Illino⋮

(See pages 64, 65 & 66)

In these huge compendiums you will find listed every magazine, trade journal and periodical published, each listed under subject matter. For instance if you want to reach farmers, look under Agriculture. You will learn the name of the publication, the name of the publisher, the address, the circulation (in most cases) and any other pertinent information needed. Copy all this information down and go home and write to these editors or advertising managers and request their "rate sheets." Armed with these you are ready to make the decision of how much money you wish to venture and where you wish to venture it.

I won't recommend any specific media, but I will tell you that I like to ferret out little known magazines which have small classified sections most advertisers don't know about. That way, my ads stand out with little or no competition. Also, the print is usually larger. (I'm against buying any classified advertising where fine, hard-to-read print is used). Your mail order buyer is usually the person over 40 whose eyes are not what they used to be. It's just plain dumb to expect him to go in search of his bifocals or magnifying glass just to read your ad. That ad may stand out like a sore thumb to you when you scan it, but to him it's just a piece of straw in a big hay stack. If you want him to see it, dye it purple and tie big pink ribbons all over it.

Of course, the universality of your subject will most determine what type of magazines your ad will pull from. If you are selling about a topic that falls under **birth**, **death** or **body**, you have a universally appealing subject and any general readership magazine should pull equally as well. Say you are advertising beauty-skin care treatment. In this case you should limit your advertising to womens' magazines, but any of these should do equally as well, if all other factors are equal.

Most advertising agencies will not even look at you, as a possible customer, if you are a beginner. But listed below are three reputable agencies that do accept small order accounts.

Chicago Advertising Agency
28 E. Jackson Blvd.,
Chicago, IL 60604

Morlock Advertising Agency
188 W. Randolph St.,
Chicago, IL 60601

Columbia Advertising Agency
P.O. Box 1285,
Richmond, IN 47374

COMPOSING A GOOD CLASSIFIED AD

In writing your classified ad, try to distill the essence of your message. Aim at being specific about what you are offering in the fewest possible words. Before me at this moment is a good example of how **not** to write an ad. It states: START YOUR OWN BUSINESS in your own home." It gives a name and address and nothing more!

What's wrong with that ad? Simple. The message does not give you a clue to what the advertiser is offering and beyond that, he is only repeating an offer that every other ad promises - - - but they give specifics . . . he doesn't. He's dead in the water!

Just below is an ad which states: *"HOW TO SELL PRINTING BY MAIL profitably. Three amazing, tested plans, free!"* Which ad would most of us be more likely to answer? The second, of course, because that copywriter told us what it is he proposes to talk about, when we send for his "free details."

Avoid generalities like the plague when writing ad copy! Don't say: It's easy to date pretty girls." Instead, say: "50 proven , tried and tested techniques to date every girl you want to."

Don't say: "Freelance photography pays well." Instead say: "1,000 tested markets that buy amateur photos."

Don't say: "Have better health." Say: "Vitamin E can help you glow, grow and live to be 100."

There's one best way to test your ad copy before you run it. Ask yourself if you would answer it, if you found it in a classified section, crowded in between hundreds of other ads. Actually place it on a page of ads and compare it to what you see there. Ask yourself what you can do to make it stand out over the others. Pay more for all caps on the first line? Buy a line of white space at top and bottom? Use a row of dollar signs for grabbing attention? Pay extra for **bold type like this**?

Don't try to be cute or flowery in your ad. Skip the histrionics. The ad must work, not so much as a rapier, as a heavy club. It must hit you over the head to get your **attention, interest** and **action** while building **desire** at the same time. That's quite an order, I'll admit . . . but that's what it takes. The time spent building such an ad should be considered "**golden hours.**" Once the ad is perfected and proven, the journey becomes a sleigh ride!

No matter how many times I stress the importance of brevity here, when you first start writing your ad you will find yourself trying to add more words . . . or reluctant to cut superflous ones. It's a natural phenomenon we all go through at first. But the painful process of word trimming must be done. Without it, you will just be losing money or, at best, trading dollars with the magazine ad answerer. It might be fun and ego satisfying but it's not profitable. Use commas as often as possible instead of *and.* You can use long words, if they are simple ones, to add size to your ad. Consider my mole & gopher ad which states: "ELIMINATE MOLES AND GOPHERS easily, quickly, inexpensively. Guaranteed method. $3.00" etc. I could have said: "easy, quick and cheap" but I would have been adding the cost of one more word and taking up less space. Besides, it would have sounded illiterate! When you learn that classified sections of some of the larger cirulation magazines can run up beyond $12.50 per word per insertion, you will soon find it quite easy to start trimming words. Of course, such prices will buy you around seven million paid circulation . . . a lot of prospects to hit at one given time. It would take our "Willy, the salesman" several lifetimes to reach that many prospects with his person-to-person sales message.

Just as with any other form of professional sales presentation, the classified ad must be made to walk the tight-rope of perfect balance. It must not say too much or too little. The graveyard of "salesmen-past" is filled with men and women who could never get the hang of saying everything that needed to be said and then . . . *"Shut upa you mouf!"* Those last famous words, I quote from my friend, Bob Park, a Korean transplant who has amassed a large fortune as sales manager for Gulf Development Corporation, makers of large electric reader signs. Bob must be listened to very closely to decipher what he is saying but he has broken every sales record with that company that ever existed! I think it is because he has that unique gift of knowing how to say everything that needs to be said during a sales presentation and then how to stand and wait for an order . . . **even if it requires 5 MINUTES OF ABSOLUTE SILENCE! I've seen him do it!**

When you get to where you can write a winning classified ad, everytime, you can get a good job in any advertising firm in the nation . . . but then you won't need a job . . . you'll be master of **your own ship!**

START YOUR OWN "IN-HOUSE" AD AGENCY

Most big mail order advertisers start their own "house" advertising agencies. They place only their own ads, of course, but in placing the order on "Ad Agency" letterhead, they qualify for a large 15% discount on every order. I postponed doing this for several seasons because it seemed dishonest. Then a friendly magazine editor-publisher suggested I do it. In his words: "You might as well . . . everybody else does." When your advertising expenditures start running $25,000 per year, you'll be saving a whopping $3,750 per year in advertising payouts.

If you are wealthy enough to afford a large advertising budget then it is also wise to hire a professional agency to place your ads for you . . . but a word of caution: test your own ads first, little by little, to be sure of what they can do. And when you do hire an agency, hire the biggest, most famous one you can find. The little "fly-by-nighters" can't or won't do a good job for you. If they were capable, they wouldn't be nickel and diming it with "small fry" like you will be as a beginner. They'd be running a mail order business of their own. When and if you hire an advertising agency, hire one that specializes in direct response business. It's a highly specialized field!

In my own life, I've long since learned a valuable lesson, over and over again. If you want an important job done and done right the first time . . . DO IT YOURSELF! . . . with the possible exception of brain surgery.

If you decide to go it alone, with your own "dummy agency," you will want to try to establish credit with a few of your favorite magazines. The first thing to do is to place continuous running orders with those publications. In advertising lingo, it's called "T.F." which stands for Till Forbid. Pay for several months in advance, less your agency commission of 15%, of course, and usually 2% more for advance payment. Next, after a few months, prepare a financial statement. List your bank, local business men with whom you do business on credit, and tell them your net worth. Do it up neatly and send it, along with a letter, asking t' magazine to extend "open account status" to you. Tell them you are contemplating heavier and heavier advertising in the future. Sometimes it is even good to send them a sample of your sales letters with an account of how well they are proving out.

Always write to the **head man,** rather than to some department head. He can always pass it back down the line, but you are more apt to get good results by starting at the top. Once you have established open account status you are in a position to expand much more rapidly. You have 30 days after publication (billing time is publication time) in which to start making returns on your advertising dollars.

ONE PICTURE IS WORTH TEN THOUSAND WORDS

My experience has proved that a profusion of well placed cartoons or pen & ink drawings will cover a multitude of misspelled words or poorly constructed sentences. In example I must make an admission. For the first nine months that I placed Writer's Utopia Formula Report on sale, it was in manuscript form. Ten pages of 8½ X 11, single-spaced, typewritten, green ink on goldenrod colored paper. There were no justified right-hand margins. In fact I ordered 1,000 reports printed before I even checked my copy for misspelled words, grammatical errors or poorly constructed sentences. The one thing I had going in my favor was that I used an ample supply of the cartoons you see in this book. When I had sold the first thousand copies at $10 each, I could boast that only two buyers had ever mentioned the plethora of grammatical errors, and I mean **plethora!** The two men who did catch it were kind enough to go through the entire manuscript and correct every error for me. One asked for refund, the other sent an additional fee to join my TOWERS CLUB, USA !

I do believe in the power of good graphics!

Be on the lookout for a good cartoonist or artist (pen & ink) who can "punch-up" your copy. Try contacting the art department of your local high school or university. Perhaps there's an art school in your town. These students love to pick up extra money assignments and most are talented enough to get the job done.

in a small, non-college town, watch the classified ads
l magazines or writer's magazines, especially. You'll
)nists who wish to work by mail. When you find your
him/her the first assignment of designing a good letter

head for your stationery and envelopes. These are vitally important if you expect to receive any business-like response from big editors to whom you may be writing for advertising favors.

Sample art from MONEY

Another, perhaps less expensive way to get illustrations is from a "ready art" house. One of the most famous is **HARRY VOLK ART STUDIO**, Box 4098, Rockford, Illinois 61110. Write and ask for their free catalog of "Clip Books." You should be able to find enough good art work here at reasonable cost to illustrate several good reports as well as advertising brochures, sales letters and coupon borders, too! Most local printers have a supply of these "Clip Books." You might ask yours to show you what he has, so you can get an idea what you want to order from VOLK.

EXPRESSIONS #535—38 art proofs. Men & women looking happy, sad, worried, surprised, etc.   **$4.75**

EDUCATION #542—22 art proofs. Teachers, students, graduates, school bus, work shop, in class, etc. **$4.75**

FAMILY #546—23 art proofs. Traveling, reading, eating, talking, watching television, etc.   **$4.75**

CONTESTS #175—15 art proofs. Realistic & humorous, beauty contest, tog-of-war, arm wrestling, etc. **$3.50**

PREPARING CAMERA - READY COPY

This subject is a complete course, in itself. Rather than try to go into it in this book, then, I am going to give you a very valuable tip. Send only $1.50 by mail, and request the latest edition of *POCKET PAL - A Graphic Arts Production Handbook* from the International Paper Company, 220 E. 42nd St., New York, N.Y., 10017. You'll receive 191 pages of detailed instructions in all phases of graphic arts. This little book was first published in 1934 and has been revised and updated ten times since then. (Ask for eleventh or a later edition. December, 1974)

Pocket Pal is small and the print is fine. If you wish to spend a little more and get a book more in tune with what we are doing as beginner-publishers, then send $4.95 to **TOWERS Book Sales Division, P.O. Box 2038, Vancouver, WA 98661**. Ask for a copy of *PRINTING IT* by Clifford Burke. The print is larger, the text well illustrated and the instructions a little easier to understand.

My only other admonition ... don't, please don't try to go to market with material you have prepared, until you have learned the finer points of graphic arts. Messy looking printed material suggests a messy mind. Nobody wants to deal with a messy, sloppy person. For instance, if you can't afford a modern typewriter or composing machine, then hire that part done by a professional typesetter. Ask your printer to supply you with proper graphic drawings to illustrate your text. He's got 'em and it's part of his duty to supply proper art when it is requested of him. If he's a real pro and has the time, he'll even offer to do the paste-ups for you, as a gesture to win your contract award on printing.

A modern IBM (or other make) composer can be picked up, at a used office equipment outlet for as little as $3,000. That may seem like a fortune to you, but believe me, it would be the best investment you ever made in your life. I can vouch for that!

IBM "Selectric" Composer

YOUR OFFER AND YOUR PRICE -- ALL IMPORTANT

This is the most critical decision a beginner must make! How much should I charge for my report? Some get an over-inflated opinion of what all that hard research and writing work was worth. (I was fully convinced I should ask $50 for this report when I saw the first one come off the printing press.) **I still think it's worth it and much, much more**, and in fact I did sell a few at that price in the beginning. But the sales were too slow in coming so I went wildly the other way, in a panic, and asked $5.24. Now the orders came pouring in faster than I could handle them, even though my sales material left much to be desired. Next I got a little bolder and upped the price to $6.45 with no appreciable change in percentage of response. Meanwhile I was hard at work developing a fancy *FREE TRIAL CERTIFICATE* and my enticing "free bonus offers" for quick answering. With this I settled on the price of $10 because that seemed to be the top price all the other "opportunity" sellers were asking. It worked very well and to date, I have remained at that figure.

You may be wondering why I go to the time and trouble of revising this book each time I order another batch from the printer. And you are right, it is **much, much harder** to revise a book than to prepare an original. But times change, and if the book is going to continue to be worth the original asking price, it must dispense reasonably current information. We try to keep this book current, simply because we have a conscience about everything we sell. It must be an **HONEST VALUE** or we don't want to sell it. There aren't too many mail order publishers who share our thoughts on this, but **Joe V. Goodman** is one who does. He is the author/publisher of *"How To Publish, Promote and Sell Your Book,* and also the owner of **Adams Press**, Chicago. His 6" X 9", 67 page, soft cover book is the perfect compliment to this one, incidentally, going into the sources of free publicity, preparing camera-ready copy for printer and much, much more. We stock this book. Ask about it. It's inexpensive and good !

But I digress! Back to pricing your reports. If you are on a limited budget, say $500 is all you can afford to "gamble" on this venture, then it's going to take several years before you can sit back and put your thumbs under your armpits. Why? Because you'll never be able to afford the big gamble of placing a full display ad, asking for up to $10 for your report. And you can never ask for more than $3 in a classified ad, and even then, it must be a darned good ad in the right classification in the right type magazine, to expect to get a flood of orders. Of course, you can run classifieds and offer to send *details,* and then send the follow-up sales letter asking for the $10 to $65 you want. That way, you just might make it to the top of the heap ahead of the rest of the pack.

MONEY - BACK GUARANTEES

I learned one very good lesson when I dropped my price from $50 to $5.24 and then upped it to $6.45 and finally to $10 ... My percentage of refund requests was far higher at the bargain-basement prices. Far more refunds! And none of those who paid the full $50 ever complained! Explain that one, please?

The lesson seems to be this: If your product is a good one, and the offer a genuine value, then you do yourself more harm than good by selling at discount prices. This may not apply in selling tangible items, but information is a nebulous commodity and an intangible item. Up to the time all the copycats in the country start selling your product at lower prices, you are wise to ask all you can get for your report or your book! How much is that? See bottom of page 58 (testing).

You who buy this book and join my **TOWERS Club Newsletter** service all with the initial purchase check, are almost never back for a refund. I like to think it is because you were pleasantly surprised to find a mail order publisher who: (1) actually lived up to his promise to mail the package the same day order was received; (2) sent what looked like a solid, workable plan, and did not try to describe it on fuzzy mimeographed kindergarten paper; (3) wrote in a manner that made you feel you were one of his good neighbors and he would want you to call him by his first name the first time you met, and finally, (4) was one of those very rare individuals Diogenes and his lamp looked all over Athens for - - - *an honest man !*

I think you reason out the obvious fact that Jerry Buchanan can't be entirely stupid. And he would have to be very stupid if he painted himself into the corner of having to publish a newsletter 10 months of every year, as follow-up material on the subject contained in this book. . . if the material in this book were some kind of a "fast-buck scheme" valuable only to the man who wrote the book. At the time of the fifth revision of this book, we were in the process of preparing our thirty-third consecutive **TOWERS Club Newsletter,** on schedule. Does that sound as though we were intending to *skip out in the night?*

Benson Barrett gets up to $65 for his writing course, without the use of direct salesmen. He does it all by mail, but he uses a series of extremely effective sales letters, mailed at regular intervals behind the first sales letter sent in answer to the first inquiry.

Eighteen years in the field of selling educational courses taught me that after you reach the plateau of $65 you must alter your approach drastically! That's when you must bring out the big guns. You raise your price from $65 to $495, at least. Then you hire commissioned salesmen, sales managers, examination graders, job placement directors, office typists, secretaries and the whole business office ball of wax. Are you ready for all that? Not yet. Maybe never. Who needs all those headaches?

How do you price a mail order product? It depends upon nothing so much as your sales ads or literature. If they are totally dynamic and overwhelmingly appealing, mouth-wateringly tantalizing, then you can ask a hundred or even a thousand times the wholesale cost to you, and they'll still sell like sun shades at the Pendleton Roundup. On the other hand, you could be selling genuine gold ingots right from the vaults of Fort Knox, at the price of pig iron, and if you had not included all the ingredients listed in the *mail-order mini-course* in the back of this book — chances are, you wouldn't sell any gold bricks at all. People are cynics these days. They need all the convincing you can present, that you are an honest merchant with a genuine value ... in fact a great bargain ... and **YOU CAN BE TRUSTED TO DELIVER IT IN GOOD TIME**, as promised in your ads.

PEOPLE ARE CYNICS THESE DAYS ! !

Now, dear reader, you might as well be told, right now ... when you enter mail order, you are mixing with all sorts of thieves, who care about nothing but a fast buck. It will be your job to convince the readers that you are <u>not</u> one of **those crooks** !

I must admit I have witnessed no evidence that lends itself to a hard and fast rule, although other entrepreneurs claim to know exactly how much you should charge to make a profit. Someone once said **"The cynic knows the price of everything and the value of nothing."** But there is often all the difference in the world between the value of a report and what you can sell it for. You must forget what you **think** your report is really worth and think only of what your advertising can ask for and expect to get for it. I once wrote what I thought to be a "pearl of great price" and fully expected to be quoted in "BARTLETT'S FAMILIAR QUOTATIONS" for it. It went: What sum constitutes fair tuition for gainful instruction? Pay the teacher his price. The knowledge he sold is yet his to sell . . . and now, yours as well."

This may be profound advice but it is *not* absolute business wisdom. Witness what is now happening to many of our major institutions of higher learning. They went on this theory from the beginning, but in latter years, (say the past 16 or so), they began gouging for all they thought the traffic would bear. They went on the assumption that **there is no monetary price too great to pay for a good education.** *They were wrong,* and as a result, many are closing their doors for the last time. They're caught in a monstrous dilemma of their own manufacture! You who are just entering the education-selling business can learn from their costly mistake. Although education is the most nebulous of commodities when it comes to pricing, it is still entirely possible to price yourself out of business! As Socrates said, **"Woe unto him who attempts to teach before the student is willing to learn."** He should have added "- - *and able to pay."*

The scientific way to set the best price lies in testing. You have 3,000 sales packages prepared, all identical except for the price. Use a direct mail approach for this one. Send 1,000 with one price; 1,000 with another price and 1,000 with a third price. Be very careful to distribute your mailing evenly. One zip code in a wealthy income district can throw your figures off a country mile. Now mail all 3,000 ON THE SAME DAY! A lapse of even **one day** can also distort your results and give you a false reading. Now compute the number of replies on each offer and total the actual number of dollars received for dollars spent in mailing each 1,000 pieces. This should give you the best price you can expect to get for your package until you change your offer. Then you must repeat the procedure. But, remember the refund factor we talked about on page 56. You can't really evaluate profit numbers until you have given your customers time to take you up on your refund offer. Aye, there's the rub, matey. Mind it.

No matter if you choose to buy space ads or just both, I think you will have a better chance of gett price for your material if you offer in the ad to se and then follow up with a powerful sales letter. Asking ey directly from the ad forces you to quote a very lov Why? Because only a full page ad can spout enough sellin, unition to create attention, interest, desire, and action! Those are the four "musts" if you expect to get more than $3 per order.

BUSINESS LICENSES & TAXES

Most cities require you to have a business license, and even though most of us do not live in an area zoned for business, the city-fathers usually look the other way if your small cottage industry is one that does not require customer traffic or employee parking on the street. City license and taxes in most U.S. cities are very minimal. Contact your state comptroller's office for requirements on state license and taxes. And It's always a good idea to furnish Dun & Bradstreet, Inc. with a financial statement, once your business is established. (See your phone bk.) Place your name on waiting list at nearest post office to rent the largest P.O. box they have. (Allows you to receive your mail many hours earlier, each day, than home delivery.)

COPYRIGHT PROCEDURE

The *copyright notice* is the most important requirement for obtaining copyright in a work that is to be published. It must be printed **on the title page or the back of the title page. No place else will be considered official** *copyright notice.*

To secure and maintain copyright protection when publishing a work, **all copies must bear the prescribed notice from the time of first publication.** The person entitled to the copyright can put the *copyright notice* on his work without obtaining permission from the Copyright Office. **NOTE: Once a work has been published without the required** *copyright notice,* **copyright protection is lost permanently and cannot be regained!** Adding the correct notice later will not restore protection nor permit the Copyright Office to register a claim. Your notice should read: *Copyright, John Doe, 1975* (or whatever year it is **first published in**). If you wish more information on different types of copyrights, send 10 cents to: **Copyright Office, Library of Congress, Washington, D. C., 20559.** Ask for the *"Circular One"* booklet, *"General Information on Copyright."* Also, while you are at it, ask for a Class application form. It will cost you $6 to file – or $10 after January 1, 1978 when new copyright laws take effect.

THE IMPORTANCE OF HAVING LETTERHEAD STATIONERY

It is amazing how much more cordial the big magazines are when answering your letters if you've written on quality letterhead stationery. Have yours prepared by a good artist and typesetter and be sure to have the design printed in a color other than black. Buy a felt tipped pen in the same color to sign your letters with. It has a pleasing effect to the reader's eye and the felt tip tends to indicate firmness of character on the part of the signer. Always keep a fresh ribbon on your typewriter if you cannot yet afford a machine with a one-time-use-only carbon ribbon.

Be thinking about a "fictitious name" for your business. It might be something like *"The House of How-To"* or *"Universal Reports"* or something equally broad and general so as to cover any number of different business situations.

A "one word" name will save you much money in advertising, since you must put your business name in each ad you run. For instance, "Mutual of New York" uses the one word *"MONY."*

A word of advice. DON'T become "J & B Enterprises" or some variation thereof. It only broadcasts to the world that you are a brand new beginner, and have a 60% chance of being out of business next week. Forget the "Enterprises" bit. Be original.

YOU DON'T KNOW HOW TO TYPE?

Then for business letters, you should hire it done, if possible, or at least buy a typewriter and labor over your own letters until they look presentable, even if you must use the "hunt and peck" system. As for your reports, there is no need to be a typist.

Say typing is not one of your skills and your hand writing is even worse. You're still very much in the writing picture because today a cassette recorder is within the affordable range for almost anyone. Your secretarial service will charge a little more, naturally, for having to stop and press the *stop* and *start* button so many times **plus** having to do ALL your spelling and grammatical and punctuation work. But the end result will make you look like a **true-blue genius** . . . and all you really supplied were the **WORDS!** If you can afford a dictating machine, it will save her a great deal of trouble (because with it, she has a foot pedal for stopping and starting your dictation). Her price per page will be adjusted downward, accordingly.

Almost every community is at least within driving distance of a major business college. I have found these to be an excellent place to find extra good typists who will work part time and for minimum scale, on piece work basis. Ask for advanced students who need to earn a little extra capital. They'll always have one or two who are eager for extra work. You might find excellent bookkeepers in the same way. For art work, find an art school and repeat the process.

THERE'S BIG MONEY IN PUBLISHING NEWSLETTERS

Some of the wealthiest entrepreneurs I know are newsletter publishers, or started out that way. Ralph Ginzburg, the "bad boy" of publishing began a little newsletter in 1973 and called it *Moneysworth*. It was 6 pages of 8½ X 11, 3 columns of 9-point type, and called "The consumer newsletter." For $5 a year one could subscribe and also receive, absolutely free, a book of *Picasso's Erotic Engravings,* or a 448-page *Home Medical Advisor* or *Stake Your Claim — How To Work The Social Security Gold Mine.* Every two weeks, there was another collosal offer if you would "extend your subscription" for another $5 spot. Many forgetful folks sent $5 a week, regularly. Today, *Moneysworth* is a 40-plus page tabloid, running *National Enquirer* a strong race for largest circulation, even though *MW* does not sell in the super markets. Ginzburg relies heavily on his genius to write a good mail order offer, and a good free bonus. All his subscribers are mail order buyers, which makes his advertising space much easier to sell. In spring of '77, price of a "Junior page - 7" X 10" went up to around $4,500 cash in advance, from $3,900. At $4 a word, his classifieds are still about the best investment I have found recently. And now, he has come out with a companion tabloid, aimed at the respectable businessman. *American Business,* 24 pages at $10 a year, bimonthly. Though printed on newsprint now, it is obvious to insiders that Ginzburg plans to aim for complete respectability this time, and we predict it will not be long before he switches the *AB* format to a slick, and aims at the jugler vein of *Barron's, Fortune,* and *Forbes.*

Newsletters serve small, fanatic-interest groups of society, from apple growers to zoological animal contractors. Since subscriptions are necessarily small, annual fees are out of sight -- from 7 to 50 times normal magazine subscription rates.

The only prime prerequisite for writing and publishing a successful newsletter is **authoritative writing and valuable timely tips**. You must have several private sources of new information and be able to put it in short, typewritten sentences, condensed to give the full story without any wasted verbiage. The usual format for a newsletter is 2 sheets (4 pages) of 8½ X 11 semi-bond paper with an attractive logo heading and typewritten editorial copy.

Many of today's top magazines started out as newsletters. Mother Earth News, Moneysworth, to name just two. Kipplinger's was the first newsletter to catch on, with the first issue out on September 29, 1923, a one-page mimeographed letter about inside information about the world market and government news. Today, they boast over 300,000 current mailing list and over a million dollars a year gross business. The magazine "Changing Times" was a spin-off of the N/L, but not a replacement. The company publishes both, plus many other booklets from time to time. If you would like to own a well written 20,000 word treatise on the subject of *"How To Start A Newsletter"* send us a check for $5 and we'll mail it out immediately, and pay the postage too. **TOWERS BOOK SALES, PO Bx 2038, Vancouver, WA 98661.**

KEEP RECORDS OF EVERY NAME, EVERY SALE, EVERY AD YOU RUN !

It shouldn't be necessary to impress you with the necessity of keeping thorough and accurate records. For one thing, you can't know which ad is paying for itself without them. For another, the tax man may want to audit you someday. For a third, those name lists are worth a sizeable second income to you. Once you build a list of 10 to 15,000, you can contact one of the better "List Houses" and place your names with them to be rented out. They charge 20% (usually) for the service, but the 80% **you get** is "pure gravy." Be very choosy in picking the company you deal with on this. Some do a much better job than others.

The day your home business grows so big you have to put on the first employee to help get the mailings out, you will know you are also ready to hire an accounting firm. **Hire the biggest and most well-known firm in the phone book,** if they'll take you. In days to come, you will see the wisdom of having a prestigious accounting firm's name stamped on your tax statements. Don't with the little guy who normally does your income ar, unless you know him personally and know him to g genius, ready, willing and able to handle ALL your ely and honestly, once he has been awakened, no matter how big you may grow. The large companies are set up for this sort of contingency, and the young man they assign to your company will stay and grow with you all the way.

WHEN ORDERING MAGAZINE ADS - -

When placing an ad order, there is a simple form to follow. You must cover all the following points in your order:

To: (publisher's name and address).

Please publish advertising of: (name of account).

In the following issues:

Rate: (From publisher's rate card).

Agency discount: (15% + 2% net ten days).

Key: (Describe how you want ad keyed).

CHECK ENCLOSED (or) OPEN ACCOUNT NUMBER _____

(Always keep a carbon of every order placed!)

See sample Insert Order Form, next page.

Always request that they publish "NO BACKING COUPONS." Always request "Checking Copies" which amounts to a free subscription to that magazine as long as your ads run there. Some magazines charge extra for "preferred position" which means toward the front of the book; on the back of cover or back cover; etc. Also, you should try to get your small space ad placed as high on the page as possible and preferably on the right hand page. Other editors will give you such "breaks" after they have come to know you and value your repeat business.

The term "TF" means that you have ordered the ad to run continuously "Till Forbid" and wish to be billed upon publication of each issue. On an open account, you then have 30 days in which to send payment with, usually, a 2% discount if paid within ten days of billing.

Lay off the heavy advertising spending during the summer months and lay it on heavy from **August through March** with a brief period of caution around Thanksgiving and Christmas time. Be sure to take into account the actual publishing **on-sale** date of a magazine. Those which are sold on newsstands usually **pre-date** their covers to give them more exposure time on the stands. For instance, their FEBRUARY issue may be the one that goes on sale during the first days after the New Year . . . NOT their January issue!

THIS IS A SAMPLE SHEET ONLY

THIS IS AN INSERTION ORDER FROM

THE JERRY BUCHANAN ADVERTISING AGENCY

1914 Stapleton Road, (P.O. Box 2038), Vancouver, WA 98661

Date Ordered
Jan 4, '77

Closing Date
Jan 5, '77

On Sale
Feb. 28, '77

PLEASE INSERT AND CHARGE TO US THE ADVERTISING AS SPECIFIED BELOW FOR OUR CLIENT: PLEASE SEND CHECKING PROOFS AND CHECKING COPIES TO BOTH AGENCY AND CLIENT.

THIS ADVERTISING ORDERED FOR FOLLOWING PUBLICATION

FREE ENTERPRISE MAGAZINE
800 - 2nd Ave.
New York, N.Y. 10017

Attn: Harriet Shatzer,
This ad as per phone call from us 1/4/77.

INSERTION DATE
Mar-Apr issue, '77

SPACE
Full page

KEY NUMBER
FE3477

POSITION
Front of book.
Right hand side.

INSTRUCTIONS:
New Velox camera-ready enclosed. Destroy old copy.

RATE
Current less agency 15% and 2% ten-day net.

Send checking copies.

THIS ADVERTISING ORDERED FOR FOLLOWING CLIENT

TOWERS CLUB/WRITERS UTOPIA
1914 Stapleton Rd.
P.O. Box 2038
Vancouver, WA 98661

OPPORTUNITY TYPE MAGAZINES

ENTERPRISE, Pat. W. H. Garrard, Publisher. Published every other month. Excellent magazine. 800 - 2nd Ave., New York, N.Y. 10017. *They don't take pd Ads anymore.*

MONEYSWORTH, Ralph Ginzburg, publisher. Published fortnightly. Excellent classifieds results usually, if your offer and ad were well written and thought out. 251 W. 57th St., New York, N.Y. 10019.

BUSINESS OPPORTUNITIES DIGEST - J. W. Straw, publisher. A monthly newsletter. Often, you can get a free placement here, if you have a worthy message. 312 Franklin St., Clarksville, TN 37040. (A sleeper. You should subscribe to this N/L anyway, if you have any entrepreneurial aspirations at all.)

MONEY MAKING OPPORTUNITIES. Don Perry, publisher. This is the best of the monthly opportunity magazines for pulling power and price of advertising. All listed below will be less profitable, but you can try them at your own discretion. MM OPS, 11071 Ventura Blvd., Studio City, CA 91604.

SALESMAN'S OPPORTUNITY, L. T. Kulikowski, publisher. Barney Kingston, Adv. Mgr. Suite 1460, John Hancock Center, 875 N. Michigan Ave., Chicago, IL 60611

SPECIALTY SALESMAN. Yale Katz, publisher. Sadako Fujii, classified editor. 307 N. Michigan Ave., Chicago, IL 60601

INCOME OPPORTUNITIES, Joe Davis, publisher. Armie Dandre, Ad director, 229 Park Ave. So., New York, N.Y. 10003

SPARE TIME, Harvey Kipen, pub'r., 5810 W. Oklahoma Ave., Milwaukee, Wisc. 53219.

IMPORTANT NOTICE

The above listed magazines and newsletters are only a few, listed in order of quality results, as we have found them to be. If the product you wish to sell does not seem to be one aimed at opportunity seekers, then the best thing you can do is spend $40 a year and subscribe to: *STANDARD RATE & DATA*, a yearly reference publication used by most of the large advertising agencies. First check your own library to see if they have it there. If not, write to: S. R. & D Service, Inc., 5201 Old Skokie Orchard Rd., Skokie, IL 60076. While you're at it, ask about their directory of mailing lists houses, also ... in case you ever decide you wish to go the Direct Mail route instead of the magazine advertisement one.

If your library does not carry S.R. & D., they may carry Ayer or Ulrich. Ask about 'em. All these directories list pertinent data on all periodicals, including ad rates, periodicity, circulation, etc.

From time to time you may have seen articles I have sold to these publications and you may be curious to know why I t... ou not to sell your work to trade publishers and then I turn ... and do exactly that! There's a method in my seeming in- ...ncy. I do a lot of advertising in these magazines and my ... my own name keyed into the copy. When I sell a full ...le to one of these publications, I get my by-line on the article - - *"by Jerry Buchanan"* placed at the top of the page under the title. If the article has merit (and I hope they all do) then I get a very expensive job of public relations done *and* **I get paid for it!** Instead of paying the publisher $1500 to buy a full page of exposure of my thoughts and ideas, **he pays me $35 to fill *his*** page with interesting, helpful material. If I have done a good job of writing; motivated or inspired the readership, then I have also told them, indirectly that Jerry Buchanan is fully qualified to help the "opportunity seeker" and this helps my ads to almost double their pull sometimes. Of course, it could work the other way around if I wrote a "dud" and, by some miracle, the editor saw fit to buy and publish it. In the pages that follow, I am going to reprint three such articles that were bought and published in national magazines in the summer and fall of 1974. Although each is slanted more toward general readership, I think they may serve to inspire you to do bigger and better things with your writing career.

The Master Salesman

By JERRY BUCHANAN

A PROFESSIONAL master salesman is one who earns his living by representing a product or service. He is the main contact between the company he represents and the prospective or established customer.

In the eyes of that customer he is the entire firm he represents. His every thought, word, deed or blunder is considered to be a true representation of the firm whose products or services he sells.

He is a statesman, a problem solver, a trouble-shooter. He is a time-saver, a profit maker for his customer as well as himself and company. He's the man or woman who sees that the right amount and quality of needed goods or services are supplied to the right people at the right time, at the right place and at a fair and equitable price.

He's a technical advisor, a business consultant, a psychologist, a veritable encyclopedia of useful knowledge, an advertising expert, a secret keeper and a carrier of useful news. He is loyal to company and customer equally; completely honest; has impeccable manners; dresses in good taste; is constantly clipping news items or technical data which he passes on to those he knows will profit from such information.

He is a father-confessor, a true friend to all who wish him to be. He calls most people by their first names, from presidents to shoeshine boys. He exudes confidence in such a humble manner that he sometimes seems shy but never unsure of himself. He never meets a stranger; is completely gregarious and may be the only person on the block who has bothered to learn the first and last name of the boy who delivers the paper—and he remembers it.

To him, remembering people's names is a way of life, and besides, there's a 90 per cent chance he was once a newspaper carrier himself. He likes everybody and completely trusts new acquaintances until they prove unworthy of his trust.

In a room full of influential people or at a social function you may notice that he is the only one who gave some time and attention to a small child or that 90 year old lady rocking in the corner, unnoticed by the others. Included in his list of close friends will be bank presidents and hobos; a millionaire financier and a widow on welfare; a minister and an atheist; a sober intellect and a funny alcoholic.

Although at times he may be improvident with the family funds, he seldom feels insecure and always seems to pay his bills on time. His quiet confidence in himself and the world around him is contagious, and while in his presence even the chronic worrier begins to feel that mankind may survive afterall.

His voice is rich and soothing. His sense of humor is quick, and when he laughs he pulls out all the stops. He is articulate; able to express any idea eloquently and extemporaneously . . . and yet, he's the world's most interested listener. He is a Master Salesman.

UPDATE REVISIONS
Please make notations of these changes in your copy of this book.

WRITER'S UTOPIA FORMULA REPORT

PAGE 53 - Harry Volk Art Studio no longer maintains an office in Rockford, Illinois. Write to: 1401 No. Main St., (P.O. Box 72), Pleasantville, N. J. 08232

PAGE 66 - Free Enterprise Magazine no longer accepts paid advertisements, as of September, 1978. They are strictly editorial, but a good source of ideas for unique entrepreneurial enterprises. Their new address is: 1212 Avenue of the Americas, N.Y., N. Y. 10036.

PAGE 34 - Rev. Kirby Hensley can be reached by writing to: 601 - 3rd Ave., Modesto, CA 95351. He offers to ordain ANYONE, free of charge, but accepts donations, and publishes a quarterly publication.

PAGE 54 - Pocket Pal keeps going up in price. Write and ask for current price. It was $2.50 at last inquiry, August, 1978.

PAGE 13 - People's Almanac does not maintain a mailing list, but the address still applies, if you wish to submit articles for sale.

PAGE 66 - Standard Rate & Data Co, of Skokie, Illinois publish many reference periodicals, used by most advertising agencies. The prices change from season to season, and the $40 price quoted here no longer applies. Send for current brochure and price list.

PAGE 85 - TOWERS Club, USA Newsletter has gone up in price. Current yearly subscription rate is $46.00. Lifetime subscription is still $250.00.

PAGES 59-60 - New copyright laws went into effect January 1, 1978. Send for latest copy of the new law at same address.

PAGE 32 - John Chase Revel's "Insider's Report" has been renamed "The International Entrepreneur's Association". Magazine sells for $35 for one year. Called "Entrepreneur", slick. Accepts paid ads.

PAGE 83 - We no longer stock Aronson book - "Writer-Publisher." We have added many other fine books not listed here. Send for our "Book Sales Division Sheet." P.O. Box 2038, Vancouver, WA 98661.

PAGE 32 - Thad Stevenson's "Opportunity Knocks" N/L is now published in Bellevue, Washington, and is well worth looking into. David Reeves has moved his CAROA N/L to Honolulu, HI, (Box 25441) Zip: 96825. Great information for exotic car buyers. He's also an auto broker. Can save you $thousands on purchase of a new car.

Opportunities...
The River of Life

by Jerry Buchanan

"Upon the Plains of Hesitation bleach the bones of countless thousands who sat down to wait, and while waiting . . . wasted and died." — *Anon.*

THE MIGHTY Columbia River runs past our town of Vancouver. I like to think of life as being like that great body of flowing water, wide and deep and always moving relentlessly towards the sea. I place my imaginary self as a swimmer in that river, trying to move upstream. When I stop stroking against the current to rest my weary muscles, I immediately begin to flow backwards and I lose the precious headway my previous efforts had gained. Life does not stop for any of us. We must grab and snatch at rest periods as best we can without losing too much momentum, if we hope to climb out of the doldrums of mediocrity. If I swim hard enough and long enough, eventually I will reach the small tributaries which feed the mighty river; the small rivers, then the high mountain creeks where I can easily wade, and stop and rest whenever I wish; contemplate the beauty that abounds where the landscape is still unabused by man. The reason? So few men ever feel that long, hard swim worth the effort.

Seek New Opportunities

Edward M. Butler once said: "Every man is enthusiastic at times. One man has enthusiasm for 30 minutes; another for 30 days; but it is the man who has it for 30 years who makes a success of life." In America, where each new day brings a plethora of new "Get Rich Quick" opportunities in the mails and magazine pages, we find it difficult to focus our attention and enthusiasm on *one goal* long enough to make it work for us. Most men and women do with opportunities as children do at the seashore. They fill their hands with sand and then let the grains sift through until the hand is empty and barren. Why not? There is always another handful of sand readily available. Most grains of sand are dull and soft, But in every handful, if you look, will be one that sparkles like a diamond. It is a microscopic gem. Opportunities are like that. When one comes along that looks like a gem to you, hold on to it for dear life. Carry it away from the sandy beach and nurture it like a precious seed. Make it grow like a diamond mine. Enclose it in a waterproof vial and secure it to a golden chain around your neck and then, start the swim up that mighty river of life. Swim for the "high country" of success where the air is still clean, the water still pure and your cabin of contentment awaits you.

How do you begin the journey? You first must banish indecision. Remember the old saw: "He who hesitates is lost" and that other, "The road to failure is paved with good intentions?" Once you have selected your own personal opportunity, put it into action with every resource you can muster. Give it everything you've got. Tear that page out of your dictionary that contains the word "impossible." Don't discuss your plan with close friends and relatives. As sure as night follows day, they will try to discourage you . . . and worse, they will probably succeed . . . in which case, neither they or you have really succeeded in anything worthwhile.

Cultivate Optimism

Learn to depend on your own God-given instincts for creativity, ingenuity, belief in the attainment of your wildest hopes and aspirations. Visualize, hourly, the ultimate goal for which you are working. Never let the mental picture become dim or faded. Hang it in a place of supreme prominence in your mental gallery. Begin a campaign of tireless research for facts about the subject you have chosen to carry you to those goals. Ask every successful man you can contact to teach you. Phone the presidents of large companies. Tell the secretary you are a long lost friend and you want to surprise him. When you get to him, tell him the truth. You are a "greenhorn" who wants to learn something he can teach. Ask him politely if he will spend a minute or two with you. Many will hang up on you, but some will be impressed . . . you thought of them and wished to learn from "the best source available in the world."

Play The Law Of Averages

As for operating capital . . . it is available in abundance to those who can convince the banker they have a plan that is workable and the persistence to see it through. If a banker turns you down, don't consider him the final authority. Keep asking until you get what you're after. Someone once said: "If at first you don't succeed . . . you're running about average." Keep on swimming upstream. When you rest, find a piling or a backwater first so the current won't carry you downstream. But don't rest too long or too often. Remember, one day of no accomplishment puts you a day behind for the rest of your life! ◄

Working with Words— the Salesman's Stock in Trade

By Jerry Buchanan, Director of Towers Club, USA

(The Original Writer's Educational Research Service)

"If a man has a talent and cannot use it, he has failed. If he has a talent and uses only half of it, he has partly failed. If he has a talent and learns somehow to use the whole of it, he has gloriously succeeded and won a satisfaction and a triumph few men ever know." Those words came not from a salesman, as we know them, but the famous novelist, Thomas Wolfe (Look Homeward, Angel) and (You Can't Go Home Again). In the short 38 years of his life he went from a love-starved, penny-pinching home to become one of the most successful authors this country has ever produced, and grew wealthy beyond his wildest childhood dreams. We don't normally think of famous writers as salesmen, but salesmen they must be, of the highest calibre. What sales manager would not be proud to sign his name to a statement like the one above?

Readers of Money Making Opportunities have one thing in common; they are interested in the business of earning more money . . . and to do that they must become word-masters. Stop the exchange of words entirely for just one week and the economy of the world would collapse. Yes, we, as salesmen, can learn much from our brothers, the writers. They, also, are salesmen and the masters of wordcraft perhaps even more so than we. Let's take pointers from a few of them here and now. Ernest Hemingway said "The first and most important thing of all, at least for writers today, is to strip language clean, to lay it bare down to the bone." Doesn't the same advice apply to salesmen? How many do you know who talk themselves into and then right out of a sale by being too verbose? Stick to your sales' formula and when you've said enough to sell yourself, stop and ask for the order. To continue beyond that point is sales-suicide.

Rudolph Flesch, eminent authority on writing and author of the best selling book, "How to Write, Speak and Think More Effectively" gives us this advice: "Do each writing (selling) job as if it were an informal talk to your reader. (Customer.) Don't start without notes—or at least specific ideas—on what you are going to say. And don't stop before you have said it. That's all! Do this a thousand times and you'll be a seasoned professional writer. (Salesman.) Couple that advice with this from Rudyard Kipling: "I keep six honest serving-men. (They taught me all I kne are What and Why How and Where an both these quotes tc of techniques and you'll never again be apt to say too little or too much, either of which can kill a sale.

Of course, it's impossible for a sales novice, using a "canned sales presentation" to apply these principles, but be assured, the one who wrote the "canned" words DID apply them, and for the very reasons given here. The presentation must have a beginning, a middle and an end, period! Most neophytes can't be trusted to stick to the formula and use their own words. It's too easy to get side-tracked, hence the kindergarten method of learning a "sales talk" by rote. But where is the dignity in parroting another person's words? It robs one of that great sense of accomplishment that comes with "putting one together all by yourself." No, if you think you want to stay in the field of sales long enough to become a top-notch master salesman, form the habit of reading—reading—reading. Another forgotten writer once said: "He who is always talking learns nothing, but he who listens will eventually have something important to say." Reading is another form of listening, just as writing is another form of talking. Send me a man or woman who reads and I will give you back a master salesman. Send me a master salesman who can talk and I will send you back a potential best-selling author. It all starts with your love of words.

MONEY MAKING OPPORTUNITIES
Page 36 SEPTEMBER 1974

...ING STARTED

...atistics show a majority of the people of this world are dreamers instead of **doers** . . . perhaps 95% of the majority, in fact. I believe this statistic will be reversed in our particular case because writers (or would-be writers) have a much higher mentality than the average person. They are more apt to have read many "success" books by men such as Napoleon Hill, Robert Collier, Elmer Wheeler, Maxwell Maltz, J. Paul Getty, Claude M. Bristol, to name only a few. If these names **are** unfamiliar to you, don't let any time elapse before correcting that bad condition in your life. You are still a blind person, groping in the dark. You don't even know, yet, the importance of setting goals and then acting with great zest and enthusiasm toward their achievement. Every great self-made man or woman who ever lived, first became **"goal-oriented!"** Right now, your first goal must be set! You must pick a subject to start researching and then you must set an exact date on which you plan to have it completed and written and ready for the printer.

* ** * ** * ** * ** *

Dear Jerry,
"I ran across a book last week while browsing at my favorite bookstore. **The Art of Readable Writing** . Turns out it's by **Rudolph Flesch** who wrote that great Reader's Digest reprint you include in your initial material - - 'Write the Way You Talk.' This fantastic book was written in 1949 but reads as though it were written yesterday. ($1.25 - Collier Bks). The most helpful part, for me, is the section on practical formulas for determining 'how easy' and 'how interesting' your writing is to read. The formulas are mechanical, but surprisingly, give a good index of how you're getting across to your reader. I recommend it highly!

Sharon G

Scottsdale, Ariz.

* ** * ** * ** * ** *

THE "CART BEFORE THE HORSE" METHODOLOGY

This may be the most important lesson I can teach you on how to organize your creative talents into a winning combination. I am sure it is completely original with me. I've never read it anyplace. Years ago, when I was doing "in the home" selling for a large business university, (I was called an enrollment counselor), I used to become frustrated because in my sales presentations, I would suddenly think of a wonderful (special feature) which I was sure would clinch the sale . . . if I could say we offered it. The frustration came from not being able to say it because we didn't really offer it. I would go back and tell the director of the school my idea ... but nobody ever wanted to change **"the way we're doing it now."** In the seed of adversity lies the full blown flower of innovation and accomplishment.

Since your new business is only the seed of an idea, at this point, you can organize it anyway you like. The best way in the world to do this is to **write a "sizzling sales letter" on the subject you plan to research and write.** It will be, at this stage, **a pure job of fiction writing!** You will tell it all the wonderful benefits to be derived from obtaining this report. Pull all the stops! Make your proposition so strong and appealing it makes **you want to dig in your own pocket to buy it!** Spend weeks on this project if you must, but don't give up until it is **overpowering in its sales appeal.** When you are satisfied, send it to every friend you know. Ask their honest and candid opinion of it's "pulling power." Offer a free bonus for an honest appraisal. You'll get it.

NOW! When it is all done to those specifications, you can set about fulfilling all your glowing promises. Research and research and write and re-write until your report lives up to every single claim you have made for it. **When this is accomplished ...you will have a winning combination! Not before.** I call this my **"CART BEFORE THE HORSE" SYSTEM.** It works for any new business venture!

† † †

A MINI - COURSE IN MAIL ORDER PROCEDURES PRINCIPLES AND PRACTICES

1. Spend 15 minutes a day, learning more about your business.

2. Try to convey an air of informality and friendliness in your literature and advertising.

3. Use a street address instead of a P.O. Box, if possible.

4. Choose a category under which many different reports can be written. (When you have written enough of them, you automatically have enough material for a book).

5. Try to think of something unique to write about and sell. The less competition, the better Don't be a copycat ! !

6. When asking for money direct from space ads, offer your product or service in the $3 to $10 bracket and always keep it in round figures. Customers are more likely to send cash if they don't have to bother about taping coins to cardboard.

7. A forty percent profit margin must be the bare minimum you can survive under. If you don't get back $3 for every one dollar you spend in advertising, give up the project.

8. Don't expect to get rich on $2 and $3 sales. They are only for the purposes of building a good mailing list of buyers, to whom you must plan to sell larger ticket items later.

9. Don't expect to make a "killing" from just one ad. Once your ad has proven itself in sales, start placing it in as many appropriate places as you can think of and afford.

10. When using space ads (display) which ask for the money now, use a size ad comensurate with the price you are asking. A large price demands a larger ad; a small price can be asked even in a classified ad.

11. It is often better to run two small ads than one large one.

12. Tailor the ad copy, illustration and headline of your ads to suit the audience of the magazine you are using.

13. Don't rush to change an ad that is pulling well. Experiment regularly, but experiment slowly. Make only one change at a time.

14. Always strive to get repeat orders quickly from buyers. The big profit in mail order is **repeat business!**

15. Small ads should be written in brief, punchy style with emphasis on facts rather than persuasion. Emphasize benefits to the customer, not to yourself.

16. Use language kept at the simplest common denominator so all will read and understand.

17. Strive for sincerity and conviction in your copy.

18. Make it easier for customers to say *yes* than to say *no*.

19. Give prospect specific directions for ordering.

20. Get a testimonial program going as soon as possible!

21. Never fail to "key" an ad, coupon or order blank!

22. Study the ads in the magazine you are considering and try to design yours to stand out from the rest.

23. The best magazines and newspapers to use in mail order are those that already carry a lot of mail order ads.

24. Newspapers are good for making fast spot-tests but for the long-haul, use monthly or bi-monthly magazines.

25. Don't be fooled by a magazine's claims of "readership." Ask for "actual circulation figures." Readership is usually 5 times the actual circulation figure. They count everyone in the family.

26. As soon as you have a successful sales campaign going, prepare a follow-up offer and have it prepared to go when your first volume of orders starts coming in.

27. From the very beginning, set up the names of your buyers on stencils or address plates. If you can't afford this, put them on multiple gummed labels. Your name list will become your most valuable property, next to your reports.

28. File your names as to: buyers; inquirers; alphebetically; by zip code area and chronologically (day, month & year). Keep on 3 X 5 or 5 X 8 cards for cross reference work.

29. If you employ an advertising agency, make double sure it is one with **heavy mail order experience!** (See page 48, this book)

30. Accept personal checks but NOT post-dated ones. Our experience has proved almost every post-dated check will ask for refund. Return them with a note of apology and don't even try to re-sell them. You don't want them!

31. Beware of the person who writes you saying he sent cash a "few weeks ago" and never received your material. It is a racket and you'll seldom find his name in your "sales" files.

32. Ship your orders the same day received. Don't hold mailings waiting for checks to clear. This could take weeks and you will have many irate customers on your hands. Most people are honest and shouldn't have to wait because a few are not.

33. Don't sit on a complaint, hoping it will go away. Answer it promptly and courteously. Give the customer the benefit of the doubt (except those who use the ploy I mentioned above).

34. If a customer sends too much money, refund the overpayment quickly. You'll win another friend and satisfied customer.

35. When you have 5,000 or more names, contact a big "List-House" and offer to rent your names to them. This can become a big source of extra income.

36. Consider writing and publishing a newsletter on your main topic of your reports. You will have a ready-made list of potential buyers from your report sales list.

37. Always try to offer a free bonus for prompt answering of your money appeals for acting "TODAY."

38. Keep a filing system on every ad you have ever run, in detail. Know what it pulled, from where and when.

39. Set up a daily record sheet and record which ads pulled what each and every day of the year. (Order 25 sheets from us - $2.30).

40. Always be looking half a year ahead in planning your ad campaigns. Start thinking about Christmas in May.

41. Get your letter head and envelopes designed and printed as quickly as possible. **They are very important!**

42. If you plan to rent a post office box, ask for the largest one available. That's positive thinking . . . besides, you may have to go on a waiting list to get one.

43. As soon as you can afford it, buy the most expensive typewriter possible . . . one with a carbon ribbon, for sharp, clear type. You will be judged not only by your words, but how they look on paper.

44. Taper off on your advertising spending in **April thru July.**

45. No list of rules will apply to every situation. Not even this one! Learn to trust in your own good horse-sense!

46. Envelope-stuffing schemes are infamous in mail order. Beware of most offers you receive in mail. Especially when your name is affixed with a small, gummed label. But read carefully all mail where your name is typed neatly on original envelope.

47. Chain letters are also a racket. Don't be taken in. Report them to your local postal inspector.

48. Make a regular habit of reading the classified ads in several mail order oriented magazines. Keep yourself informed of what other entrepreneurs are up to. You can't improve on the competition if you don't know what they are doing!

49. Plan to plow most of your earnings back into more advertising for the first year or two. The more you put in, the more you take out.

50. Using dollar $igns in your literature and ads is a sure give away that you are a rank amateur. Don't do it.

51. Using *"Enterprises"* in company name does the same thing.

52. Don't ever have the price actually printed on your product. You may have to change price before all are sold.

53. Don't quote price in sales letter. Include a separate coupon in envelope, on which price is quoted. Same reason as above.

54. Find out where your local printers buy their paper. Set up a wholesale buying deal with supplier and save money.

55. Join **TOWERS Club, USA,** if you haven't already !

END OF MINI - COURSE
† † †

There are those who stop looking for work as soon as they have found a job.

--- CONCLUSION ---

Yes, you'll make some mistakes, even with all I've taught you! It's inevitable. But remember, I made it pay big without the help of a book such as this, and I must admit, I made darned few mistakes, at that! Common sense goes a long way to fill in where education fails to show her beautiful head.

As long as you maintain that high degree of enthusiasm we talked about and **put action where there were formerly only dreams,** you **must succeed and gain a satisfaction few men ever experience** . . . and of course, throughout this book, I hope you realized that where I used the word *men,* I was limited by a fault in our basic language structure. I meant *men* and *women!*

TOWERS CLUB, USA

Although I've tried to think of every situation and problem you may run into, there is still much, much more for you to learn. **I still learn new and valuable lessons about direct response every single day I'm alive!** Since I can't recall this book every week and add to it, the new "wrinkles" I've learned, you'll either have to go the rest of the way on your own . . . or subscribe to my TOWERS CLUB, USA Newsletter. With the newsletter device, I am able to bring my followers up-to-date on every new thing I have learned each month. **And, did you know, money paid out for subscriptions to publications about the business you are actually engaged in are fully tax deductible?** Once you've written and sold your first copy, you are technically **"in the trade."**

My good and long-time friend **Doris Heyler** of Chehalis, Washington (once a New York fashion model; now the wife of a successful gentleman-farmer) calls her seeds **"God's little factories."** It is a source of constant amazement to her to plant a miniscule seed in fertile soil and watch it develop into something green and wonderful.

I would like you to think of this book as a **seed - - one of "God's little factories."** Between us, (I, by writing and you, by reading) we have planted this seed in the fertile soil of your mind. How well it grows and what it becomes will depend almost entirely on how well you tend your own garden. By subscribing to my

...sletter, you will be, in effect, hiring me to stop by your place once a month (sort of the visiting horticulture specialist) to see how well your seed is developing and to give timely advice as it is needed. I promise you my Newsletters are quite a bit **above average** in quality, content and quantity of useful information! In other words, **the price is 30% lower than the national average for newsletters while the content is at least 30% above that same average!**

> *"The man who will use his skill and constructive imagination to see how much he can give for a dollar instead of how little he can give for a dollar, is bound to succeed!"*
> ... Henry Ford

My Club members like to keep in touch with me by mail. They often send me newspaper or magazine clippings on subjects that have to do with our common cause, which I in turn publish in digested form in our Newsletter. The idea behind this is that what appears in your newspaper probably does not appear in mine. There are 73 news feature syndicates in this country all turning out volumes of valuable information daily. But no one newspaper can possibly afford the cost or space to run all the "How-To" articles available. In fact the average newspaper picks up only about *one percent* of the interesting feature articles available on any given day. Thus what you read in our N/L will be something you had a 99% chance of missing in your own daily reading. **Another very valuable service we provide is a fast way to build a list of favorable testimonial letters to use in later advertising copy.** By advertising your new reports in our N/L at reduced price, our members know that you are expecting them to write a critique of your work, good or bad, if they buy it. So you'll get many letters of evaluation. If they're good - **BINGO!**

None of us is as smart as all of us.

As each member announces the completion of a new report, you will be one of the first to know about it! You may want to purchase it or perhaps the two of you will agree to trade reports. Either way, you will be one of the first to gain valuable new, indepth knowledge. Soon your store of new and useful "how-to" information is bound to make you one of the wisest persons in your community, city or state. Think what a wealth of useful information you will be able to pass on to your children or family. Each report will be a digested condensation of thousands and thousands of research manhours by hundreds of intelligent and talented writers! **Knowledge is indeed wealth!** Given a choice between money and knowledge, the wise man would take knowledge everytime . . . BUT . . . darn it, there are too many college educated men and women walking around with holes in their soles, right here in America -- breadbasket of the world. Yes, we need knowledge, and **TOWERS** will give us that. **But it will also give us the vehicle by which we can grow more financially secure by doing what we like to do best . . . work with words!**

ASSOCIATE RESEARCH EXCHANGE PROGRAM

On pages 11 thru 13 of this book we talked about modern research methods. Here is another we invented ourselves. If you become a member of **TOWERS Club**, you can, if you wish, have several hundred intelligent people keeping their "reading-eye" peeled for good articles about subjects that interest you. It's called our **AREP (Associate Research Exchange Program)**. For the additional sum of $10 per year, you can have your *profile* and *3 research requests* published in our quarterly roster sheet. The lists are mailed to all who are signed up and have returned their filled-in **Personal Data Sheet.** The idea is to send good clippings to those persons listed in the roster who have indicated an interest in a particular subject. They, in turn, are supposed to be particularly on the alert to find an article of similar worth or value or interest on one of your own listed main-interest subjects. The idea works like *"Casting your bread upon the waters."* Nobody pays anybody anything, in actual money ... but we do try very hard to repay those who have shown us a kindness, AND ... it's a very good way to meet new friends!

It has been wisely observed that most people consider themselves lucky if they find even one really true friend in a lifetime. With our AREP, you are allowed to meet hundreds of people who share similar age, educational background, occupations, hobbies, religions, special interests, and even astrological signs. We can't guarantee you'll meet one of those rare "true friends" but you must admit, the chances are increased a thousand fold.

I can tell you from first hand experience, that the brightest part of my day, Monday thru Saturday, is the opening of my mail* Letters from every corner of the earth. Warm, friendly letters, usually with interesting clippings about things I have displayed an interest in (self-publishing success stories, new religions, water-witching, and bio-rhythms). What would be your three research-request topics, if you were to join AREP?

*Note: Jerry's mail has grown so voluminous that he finds he often has to ask the correspondent to forgive him for not being able to write personal answers anymore, as he used to. But that doesn't mean he doesn't still enjoy receiving those wonderful letters ... especially the ones that tell how much they liked this book and the newsletters. The most interesting letters are reproduced in TOWERS Club Newsletter, along with Jerry's answers. (Beverlee).

WHEN WE BUY A BOOK

Old Ben Franklin said: **An investment in knowledge pays the best dividends.**" Anytime I get an opportunity to buy for a few dollars, a money-making plan the seller has spent a fortune and many years perfecting through trial and error - - I buy and get far the better part of the bargain! Even if I never use the knowledge, I am far richer for knowing I **could if I ever wanted to!** I think Mr. Franklin would applaud my thinking on that.

If the author was thoughtful enough to trim the words to a minimum without leaving anything to my guess-work, then I feel the value received was at least doubled! To me, a book filled with well-written, authoritative "How-To" information on **any subject** is a **priceless possession** and I treasure it with my life. Ask to borrow my car, my boat, even my wife before you ask to borrow one of my treasured "How-To" books. You'll have a better chance.

I wasn't raised in a particularly intellectual nor academic environment. My family was "just ordinary." Like Jim Bishop, whose father was a policeman, mine was a fireman. The credit for any level of proficiency I may have gained in the field of literary endeavor must go to those two wonderful high school teachers I mentioned (who taught me the love of words) and to the myriad authors whose minds I "picked-clean", as I feel they intended me to when they put their knowledge on paper and had it published. Collectively, they taught me all I know . . . and I am deeply grateful to each and every one of them. I shall continue to read and study and learn until the day I leave this body.

I feel confident that most who read this book will feel, as I do, it is uniquely simple and simply unique. If it makes me a lot of money, that will be as it should be. That's what the American free-enterprise system is all about, isn't it? You find a need and a way to fill it. Do only this and it is inevitable that you will be generously rewarded in coin of the realm. What is even more extraordinary is that this is the **only book I have ever known about where the author does not leave you at the end, to fend for yourself!** I offer a continuity and a "running sequel" in my **TOWERS CLUB Newsletter service.** As I learn more, you who **join** will be the first to learn what it is and how to use it! As the trends in buying and selling; in dollar fluctuation; in publishing; in writing styles, and in advertising fashions change, you will be **the first to know!** As our club members, one by one, become wealthy, you will be **the first to read exactly how they did it!**

YOU MAY NEED ONE EXTRA INGREDIENT

As we promised in the beginning of this little book, we have covered the most ground possible in the least possible amount of your time. We trust we moved along quickly enough to hold your interest, so that you were able to complete the reading at one sitting. That always seems important to me, in reading a technical book of any kind. Otherwise, one is too apt to forget important steps gleaned from the first segment of reading . . . steps the author had intended for you to fix firmly in your mind as you progressed. If the second segment of reading is too many days behind the first, it's quite likely your major purpose in buying this book in the first place has been defeated. Let's hope not. You can always go back and read it again...and most of my customers inform me they have read this book through from 4 to 8 times, and are still finding important points they had missed in all previous readings.

And yet, you should bear in mind that I did not have this book or any other book like it, when I first launched into this business. What I did have was SALESMANSHIP know-how! A most important ingredient in this formula. Strangely enough, I had almost no experience in advertising copywriting . . . but when you come right down to it . . . what is advertising except good salesmanship applied to a good product?

All the same principles apply. Find a superior product, one you are sold on yourself. Find the area where there are the most potential buyers. Saturate that area with a well written sales story, and ask for the money in such a way that it is easier for the prospect to say "yes" than to say "no."

Well, that all sounds easy, when you say it fast and walk away. Actually, it isn't all that easy, for someone who has never been in a position of having to earn his entire income from applying those principles and practices, as I was for 18 years. (No salary whatsoever. Straight commission and I even had to pay my own traveling expenses!) You learn the psychology of what makes people buy, in a hurry, when you choose to become a full-commissioned salesman. And that's precisely what you are doing when you decide to become a mail order entrepreneur on a full time basis.

KNOWLEDGE IS POWER

Don't worry, I'm not going to let you go until I'm c
you are not going to stumble and fall. That's why I have
my shipping-room shelves with several priceless, hard-
books on the two subjects - - selling and advertising - - a₁
eral others on the mechanics of self-publishing/marketin,
time goes on, some of these books may become unavailable, ...u
new ones may be added to our stable. But for now, I want you
to know I've spent many months locating, ordering and stocking
them for resale to my readers. This means that every book you
will eventually want to own if you stay in this business, is available from ONE SOURCE. And that's doubly nice when you remember that TOWERS Club, USA is famous for being the fast-
est order-fillers and shippers in the mail order industry today !
It's simple. We want to continue to be your mail order supplier.

The following are a current list of the books we most recommend as a bibliography to be added to your library as time and
money will allow:

Successful Direct Marketing Methods - Bob Stone	$19.95
Tested Advertising Methods - John Caples	$10.95
Lazy Man's Way To Riches - Joe Karbo	$10.00
How I Made A Million In Mail Order - E. Joe Cossman	$ 8.95
My First 65 Years in Advertising - Max Sackheim	$ 5.95
Printing It - Clifford Burke	$ 4.95
The Writer/Publisher - Chas. N. Aronson	$ 7.95
How To Publish, Promote & Sell Your Book - by Joe V. Goodman	$ 3.25
How To Publish Your Own Book - L.W. Mueller	$ 4.95
How To Start Publishing Newsletters - Stevenson	$ 5.00
Mail Order Moonlighting - Cecil C. Hoge, Jr.	$15.00
Winning In Mail Order - G. R. Paro	$10.00
How To Start Your Own Business on a Shoestring and Make Up To $100,000 A Year - Tyler Hicks	$ 9.95

(In Continental U.S., add 65 ¢ for each book   shipping & handling please.)

Any of above books may be ordered from this page. Simply enclose check in proper amount and add 65 ¢ per book, shipping &
handling charges. All books will be shipped special 4th class
book rate, same day order is received. All foreign orders must
be paid for with checks or money orders which specify "Pay in
U.S. Funds." Air mail charges, for overseas destinations are
often as much as the price of the book, itself. So if you live
overseas and order a book shipped airmail, please double the
amount of your payment and specify "Air Mail."

THE COPYWRITER'S CREED (as we teach it).

A headline that grabs the curiosity.
A sub-head with startling promises.
Tell who's writing ad, & qualifications.
Create interest, then desire to own.
Confirm value with good testimonials.
Make offer they can't refuse.
Make money-back offer believable.
Promise super-fast delivery.

IF YOU LIKE US - - JOIN THE INNER CIRCLE

The day you compose, test and finally place a full page ad in a national magazine, that's the day I'll know another of my students is ready for the big time. When you're ready to try that, you should do two things. (1) Break out this book and review the copywriter's creed above, and (2) send me the proper amount to buy into my Inner Circle at TOWERS Club. The present cost is $250, which buys my personal consultation service AND a life-time subscription to my newsletter, as well. But that price may go up at any time, so check with my office for details. Of course, you are welcome to join Inner Circle before that, if you wish to. You may deduct the amount you just paid for TC subscription from the total fee, if you are a brand new subscriber.

You no longer feel like a square peg in a round hole.

HOW TO ORDER

Hi! I'm Beverlee Buchanan, Office Manager and Chief order-taker. If you wish to subscribe to our Newsletter (which is the same as joining our TOWERS CLUB, USA . . . or if you wish to purchase books from our Book Sales Division . . . or if you wish to receive our quarterly AREP (New Member Roster Sheets) --- I am the girl you'll want to write to.

Just drop a note and let us know what it is you wish to have shipped and let me take care of the paper work. I'll see to it the order is shipped on the same day we receive it (except weekends, of course).

Mail your check in proper amount to below address. Oh yes, the price of one year's subscription and Club membership is currently $24.00. If you add the AREP, that's $10 extra. ($34).

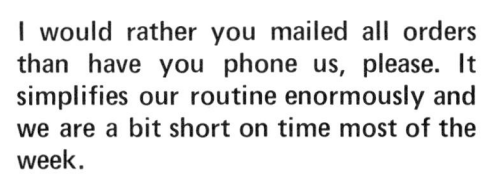

I would rather you mailed all orders than have you phone us, please. It simplifies our routine enormously and we are a bit short on time most of the week.

       Thanks for your orders and
       your understanding.

Beverlee Buchanan, Office Manager
TOWERS Club, USA,
Post Office Box 2038, (Dept.WUF),
Vancouver, WA 98661 (U. S. of A.)

PUBLISHED BY :

TOWERS CLUB U.S.A.

Post Office Box 2038,
Vancouver, Washington 98661